SURVIVING BEYOND
HAPPILY EVER AFTER

JOAN BUSICK

JR | JAMES-ROBERT
P | PUBLISHING
Scottsdale, Arizona

SURVIVING BEYOND
HAPPILY EVER AFTER

by JOAN BUSICK

Published by:

JR | JAMES-ROBERT
P | PUBLISHING

James-Robert Publishing Company
15838 N. 62nd Street
Scottsdale, AZ 85254-1988 U.S.A.

Cover design by Jim Kramer
Illustrations by Dona Lee Nill
Author photo by Kate Porter

ISBN 1-888540-50-8 (pbk.)
Printed in the United States of America.

Publisher's Cataloging-in-Publication

Busick, Joan.
Surviving beyond happily ever after / Joan Busick. — 1st ed.
p. cm.
ISBN: 1-888540-50-8
1. Widows—Life skills guides. 2. Divorced women—Life skills guides. 3. Decision-making—Handbooks, manuals, etc. 4. Self-help techniques.
I. Title.

HQ1058.B87 1999 646.7'0082

This book is dedicated
to all women
who have been there.

ACKNOWLEDGMENTS

We all need cheerleaders. We all need people on our own personal team who push us forward, provide us with unconditional encouragement, and convince us that we can succeed at anything. An enormous hug and thank you to the special cheerleaders in my life: Barbara and Jim Kramer, my mom and dad, for building the foundation, setting the standards, and continually reinforcing them along the way. Larry Goodwin, my husband, for respecting who I am and where I came from, and encouraging me to spread my wings. Jesse and Cody Busick, my boys, for sharing the journey, and for constantly reminding me that I am "awesome." Todd Goodwin, Larry's son and my good friend, for making me computer literate and getting me out of innumerable technical dilemmas. Barbara McClure, gentle editor and friend, for her eloquent encouragement and input. Diana Herrington, respected psychotherapist, for her invaluable insight into sociological influences on women. Jim Spencer, publisher and overall good guy, for putting the pieces together. And last, but so very important, my women clients from whom I have learned so much. Thank you for sharing with me, so honestly, your dreams and fears and feelings. Your names have been changed for this book, but you all know who you are, and how much you mean to me.

CONTENTS

FOREWORD

Most of us never expected to be on our own. Yet, there are over 22 million women in the United States today who are either divorced or widowed. As our population continues to age, this number will grow.

We were raised in a society that taught women to believe in Happily Ever After—to believe that all we had to do was focus on finding that perfect man and he would make our dreams come true. The messages were so subtle that even the brightest of us didn't notice. We placed limited value on our own intelligence and had little confidence in our ability to make decisions. And, as Joan Busick explains in this remarkable book, society did not bother to prepare us for one of life's more probable story lines.

It is safe to say that very few of us have *not* "been there." We have all relied on someone else to "fix things" and to make the important decisions. But then, quite unexpectedly, that someone else is not there anymore, and we are at a loss as to what to do next. This isn't how it was supposed to be.

In *Surviving Beyond Happily Ever After,* Joan explains, using her own life as an example, how women have bought into society's myths. She then proceeds to shatter these myths and replaces them with simple but effective skills to make our lives happier, more fulfilling and more powerful than we could have ever dreamed. She explains how decision making is the key to survival, how it is the key to gaining control of our lives. And she reminds us to never put ourselves down for who we are or where we have been.

I had the good fortune of meeting Joan while embarking on a new business in the publishing field not quite five years ago. At the age of 58, I became a business owner for the first time in my life. Blind luck or heavenly angels must have blessed me as Joan became my accountant, advisor and very special friend. She is a rare combination of a realist who still believes we can make dreams come true. Thus, she encouraged me to follow my own dream, tempering it with sound advice.

The message Joan shares with us in *Surviving Beyond Happily Ever After* is that we can, and must, take responsibility for our own lives, our own decisions, our own happiness. Her book is informative, highly readable and a tremendous service to women. I encourage you to not only read this book, but share it with a friend.

—Barbara McClure
Editor & Publisher, *The Desert Woman*

Part I

Gender Evolution

IN THE BEGINNING

To clearly understand who you are, and where you are, at any point in your life, you need to have a solid understanding of where you came from. So I'd like you to do something for me. Settle into the most comfortable chair you can find, and do your best to free your mind of today's problems and to-do lists. Now . . . think back and try to remember. Think back to the days when you were small and life was so very simple. Think back to the days of make-believe and dress-up, of tea parties and doll houses, and knights in shining armor. Remember how safe and uncomplicated life seemed to be? Think back to the bedtime stories that gradually evolved, as years passed by, into favorite love songs played over and over again on the radio. Did you just naturally assume, back then, that life would always be this good? Did you believe, if only subconsciously, that all you had to do was follow the path unfolding before you and you would be guaranteed Happily Ever After? I admit that I did.

Like so many other young women, I was the product of a society that intentionally raised women, generation after generation, with this simplistic, fairy tale philosophy towards life. We were raised with stories of Cinderella and Snow White. As we grew older, we progressed to romantic comedies where Doris Day always ended up with Cary Grant or Rock Hudson.

Tammy always married the rich bachelor next door. The Good Life, if nothing else, was always predictable. We truly believed that Prince Charming would sweep us off our feet and take care of us forever and ever. He might arrive in the form of a salesman or cowboy, but he would still be Prince Charming.

Let's face it, life *was* uncomplicated back then. Everyone knew their place in society, and everyone knew what was expected of them. Women were raised to be wives and mothers, and men were expected to assume the role of protector and breadwinner. And we thought that this is how it would always be. But then, to everyone's surprise, and without much warning, a decade came along that turned everything upside down. A decade that caused so many of us to re-evaluate all that had once seemed so permanent. Think back and try to remember. I'm talking about the 1960s.

If you look back at modern history, most decades never really acquired a personality all their own. Yes, they may have been an accumulation of years in which, in any one random year, a special event or catastrophe altered the course of our society or world. But taken as a whole, to be acknowledged for a particular impact, a lot of decades just quietly passed on by.

But then you have a decade like the '60s. WOW. Talk about dynamic! If you look back on the events that took place during that ten-year period, it is almost inconceivable to think that so much change and upheaval could have taken place in such a short period of time. Assassinations of presidents and leaders, a war that disillusioned the young, and a kaleidoscope of events brought an end to our modern-day version of Camelot and gave birth to a questioning of authority.

Like most people, you probably remember where you were on a given day when one of these pivotal events took place. I remember where I was the day that JFK was shot. I also remember sitting in a living room with a spellbound group of friends watching draft numbers being drawn on national television. I remember the feeling of disbelief when my brother-in-law's number was picked, and the jumble of emotions when he was later disqualified for health reasons. Just mentioning the '60s to most people brings to mind a collage of colorful—or tragic—reminders: psychedelic posters from Haight-Ashbury, bell bottoms and peace symbols, the sounds of the Age of Aquarius from the cast of *Hair.* (All right; I'll be honest. I still have my peace symbol necklace purchased on a street corner in San Francisco. I wouldn't give it up for anything.)

Nothing seemed sacred anymore. As the decade gained momentum, the younger generation began to question everything: the Establishment, long-held traditions, and an unspoken class system. Blacks demanded equality; the young demanded to be heard. Yet women, as a whole, pretty much continued to watch in relative silence. But they did begin to question, and they did begin to stir. And basically ponder, "What about us? Aren't we somebody?" Until finally, at the end of this tumultuous, anything-goes decade, they let loose and ran kicking and screaming, with burning bras, into the 1970s and the evolution of the female gender.

Women took the discontent of the '60s and applied it to their own place in society. Leaders of this "women's movement" began to emerge and demand that the world pay attention. They no longer wanted to be secondary citizens. They no longer wanted to be merely subservient supporters of men. They wanted equality. They wanted respect. And they wanted it now.

For some, it was a revolution. For others, no more than a mild awareness. But, without a doubt, the messages were evcrywhere. And even if you didn't like the messenger, you couldn't help but ponder the message. Some were subtle; some were in-your-face. Women spoke of inequalities, lack of voice, lack of respect. They debated their place in society, business and politics. They took sides as to whether they should march on Washington D.C. or wrap themselves in Saran Wrap to please their husbands. And although society passionately debated, and definitely did not agree upon what a woman's role was or should be, there did seem to be a universal, newfound understanding that there were options, that women did have choices.

This noisy, new awareness forced women, in general, to privately ponder their own existence, to think about who they were and how they fit into the world around them. They were told that they, in fact, could be independent, intelligent members of society. They were told that they had the ability, and, yes, even a responsibility, to make decisions that directed the course of their own lives. They did not have to passively plod along a path chosen for them by others.

How women individually responded to these messages depended upon a large number of factors: their upbringing, their financial situation, their education, their personality. Their overall contentment, or lack of contentment, with where they were in life. And their age. Especially their age.

For many of these women, age played a profound role in how they reacted to this new way of thinking. And for obvious reasons. With youth comes curiosity, a sense of rebellion and a desire to change the world. It seems that endless possibilities lie before you, all at your beck and call. You're still deciding what fork in the road to take; you're not yet set in your own ways. So the concept that you now have this added power to voice yourself in society, or at least in your own private world, was clearly an idea eagerly absorbed by the young.

But, as we all know, with age comes complications, and commitments to other people. Suddenly it's not just YOU, it's US. Over time it is not rebellion that matters, but comfort and status. Forks in the road are passed by, and routines are established. So messages being shouted at you about demanding equality, and about the shaking of foundations upon which you've already started to build your adult life, are not as easily accepted now as they might have been when you were younger. The messages may cause you to pause and think, and you may agree with the overall concepts, but your life will continue on as usual, simply because it IS your life.

I guess most of us just assumed that we would live happily ever after . . .

THE RETURNING WOMEN

It seems so obvious now, but back then it never occurred to many of us that climbing out of a hole could take so much longer than jumping into one. That regaining control of our lives could be such a slow, slow process.

It is now time for me to confess: I was not part of that first wave of women from the '60s who figured out that they had to take responsibility for themselves. To this day, I honestly am not sure why. And I've thought about it a lot. Because looking back, I had all the right statistics. I was young, well-educated, and came from a middle class family filled with culture and high standards. A college degree was expected of me. My father was an architect and my mother owned a secretarial school. But somehow, by the time the messages got to me, I had already passed too many forks in the road. I was already headed down a given path.

Thinking back, it seems like such a long time ago. In my second year of college I met my future husband, Chip. I married him, I guess, simply because he asked me to. He wanted to move to a different part of the state, I was bored with my classes and had no real direction in college, so I dropped out and followed him there. Soon after that I had one baby, then another, because, again I guess, that's just what you did. Our lives became busy, as well as increasingly hectic, and before too long survival and comfort became the main focus of my attention.

At the time I didn't realize it, but my situation was far from unique. There were so many other women like me who didn't really think about where they were going, but who just quietly followed a path set by others. Yes, we heard the messages. And yes, some were subtle and some were in-your-face. At times we even debated their merit. But somehow we didn't really think that they applied to us. Maybe it was because we smugly thought of ourselves as being "settled." We truly thought we had *chosen* the course we were following, and besides, we were too busy taking care of our families to deal with the questioning of our own existence.

So the years went by. And some of us found contentment in the roles we filled, while others gradually felt a rumbling.

Personally, I remember being slightly overwhelmed by the role of motherhood, but found great delight in the newly-acquired skills of cooking and gardening. During the day I occasionally taught bread-baking classes to raise a few extra dollars for groceries, and then settled into a small part-time bookkeeping job. The little bit of extra income did help, but we never could seem to quite make ends meet. Like so many other young couples, financial struggles were a regular part of our everyday life. Unfortunately, happiness was not. And while I thought at the time that I was doing my part, in reality, I realize now, what I was really doing was waiting for my husband to make us rich and happy. And I kept waiting. And waiting. Until, as the years passed by, I reluctantly had to admit (only to myself) that we were not getting anywhere close to rich, and I was far from happy.

You must understand that this was not an easy revelation to acknowledge. Like a lot of other young women, I had always assumed that of course I would make the right decisions in life, and that, of course, I would be happy. We were not prepared for anything else. An acknowledgment of discontent, of being out of place, opened up unknown territory that we hadn't ever considered. And like these other women, I was sure that there had to be some mistake. This was not how my life was supposed to go.

Now, don't get me wrong. Most of us had never been on welfare; most of us had never been physically abused, or homeless, or, for that matter, had a life-threatening disease. We just simply weren't where we were supposed to be. It's not that we had made *bad* decisions in life; it's just that we hadn't *made* decisions. We had merely let life happen to us.

For the majority of us, this realization was gradual. But when it hit, it hit hard. Because if, for most of your life, you have let others make decisions for you, you are bound to feel that you have no ability to change your own circumstances. You have feelings of resignation and helplessness, and you feel that the situation you are in will go on forever.

The beginning of my own personal awareness came around the time of my ten-year high school reunion. (Sounds like quite a cliché, but it's true.) I guess the idea of seeing people who knew you "back when" tends to make most of us do a little self-evaluation. All my old friends were thrilled to see me again. Gosh, I looked great, and what had I been doing for the past ten years?

To my surprise, I found myself embarrassed; I was humiliated. I found that I didn't want to tell these people who knew me when I was so full of potential that I was just a part-time bookkeeper, that my husband was a horseshoer (really), that we spent most of our time raising two kids and trying to make ends meet. I discovered just how disappointed I was with my life. Yet at that moment, it still didn't occur to me that I could do anything about it.

But every so often we have the good fortune of having the right catalyst, or message, presented to us at the right time. Mine came in the form of a book. From my mom. She was reading some rather esoteric, thought-provoking stuff at the time, and sent me this book entitled *The Nature of Personal Reality* by Jane Roberts. I admit that I only read a few chapters, and to this day have not finished the rest of it. Nor do I remember most of what I read. Except one passage. That changed my life. It went like this: "The realization that you form your own reality should be a liberating one. You are responsible for your successes and your joys. You can change those areas of your life with which you are less than pleased, but you must take responsibility for your being."

Whoa! I read this passage, and reread it. I put the book down, thought about it, and read it again. Then thought about it some more. Until suddenly the light went on. I was responsible for my happiness. NOT my husband. I was able to change those areas of my life with which I was less than pleased. NOT Chip. I began to realize that I was the only person who could do something about my life. No one else could. And you know what? It scared the hell out of me. But it was time I took responsibility for my being.

This was the beginning of my own cautious, and painful, process of thinking about who I was and who I wanted to be. Where I was and where I wanted to be. Chip and I began to talk—cautiously and painfully—about what was wrong, and how we were going to fix it. Quite honestly, a lot of our conversations would start with him saying, "So what is it you want?" and me saying, "I don't know!" (I never said it was a streamlined, easy process.) We eventually determined that there was something I needed to finish. I had this desire to make something of myself, to finish something I had started. I needed to go back to school.

As a bookkeeper earning $5 an hour, I was responsible for paying the bills of the company I worked for. One of the regular bills was from an accounting firm. I would look at the charges for services, such as preparing payroll returns that I knew how to prepare, and think, "I can do that. They're charging $50 an hour and I can do that. Why can't I earn $50 an hour?" Chip and I agreed that maybe I had some untapped earning potential. Just maybe, I could be a certified public accountant.

I remember going to a birthday party in the local park for one of my kids' friends. Someone pointed out Billy's dad standing over by a tree and casually mentioned that he was a CPA. The poor guy never knew what hit him. I had him cornered in a minute, asking him every possible question I could think of: What exactly did it take to become a CPA, what kind of tests did you have to pass, how many years did it take, and by the way, what exactly did a CPA do? I cornered and talked to just about anyone I could think of who knew anything remotely connected with the accounting profession, until I finally came to the decision that it was exactly what I had the potential to do.

And so we rearranged schedules, my wonderful dad agreed to pay for my tuition, and I headed back to school. Junior college first, because I had heard that it was more user-friendly than four-year universities and, besides, I had to make sure that I actually could remember how to take a test and pass a class. I knew that I would be at least ten years older than the average "just out of high school" student, and that in itself was intimidating. Without a doubt, that first day would be terrifying.

For one thing, what did one wear to school now? I mean, just looking at the kids walking down the street made me aware of the fact that dress codes had changed a lot in the past ten years. For that matter, I got the distinct feeling that there no longer *were* any dress codes.

Then there was that other problem, so much more important than what to wear: my boys. What would I do with them? How would they get along without me? I was starting my classes during summer, which unfortunately meant that they were in the middle of their summer vacation and used to my being there. After much debate, Chip pointed out the fact that he was a parent, too, and since he was self-employed and basically set his own schedule, they could hang out with him while I was off on my new adventure.

So my big day arrived. I managed to find my classrooms on time, and no one seemed to notice that I wasn't eighteen, much less pay attention to what I was wearing. Upon returning home at the end of the day, my boys ran to greet me with a look on their faces that said "Thank God, we're saved!" But by the fifth day upon my return home, I remember my youngest son, Cody, looking up from the truck he was playing with and saying, "Oh, hi Mom," and then returning to his game. At that point I knew we would survive.

Once this new life settled into a routine and I personally settled down long enough to look around me, I was amazed at what I found. There they were. Everywhere. Women just like me—older, with kids, with husbands, or ex-husbands, with the same insecurities and same need to have a second chance at an opportunity they passed up the first time around. You know, they even had a name for us. We were known as the Returning Women.

Not only did we have a name, but we acquired a reputation. We wanted an education, and we wanted it bad. Unlike the eighteen-year-olds just out of high school who were there primarily because that's what you *did* after high school, we really, really wanted to be there. We wanted to learn. We wanted to make something of ourselves. And probably for the first time in most of our lives, we had made a specific decision about the direction we wanted our lives to go. We no longer were merely following the path laid out by others.

We paid attention in class, weren't afraid to ask questions, studied hard, and, in most cases, got top grades. In turn, these grades reinforced in us the knowledge that we were worth something, that we had the ability to set goals and achieve them. And that feeling of achievement was nothing short of awesome.

For my part, I thrived in college this second time around, and after taking all the required classes I possibly could at the junior college level, transferred to a four-year university, California Polytechnic State University in San Luis Obispo. I went on to earn my Bachelor of Science degree in Business Administration, with a concentration in Accounting, was hired by a local CPA firm, earned my accounting certification and, of course, lived happily ever after.

Well, okay, so it wasn't quite that simple.

PILLOW TALK REVISITED

Returning Woman's Reality Check #101: Just because you're doing something that you really want to do, something that you know is right, doesn't necessarily mean that it's going to be easy. Getting through school was, without a doubt, one of the toughest things most of us had ever done.

For starters, we suddenly had one more activity—studying—to juggle with all the other activities of the day. We rearranged priorities and then found our existing relationships strained by our newfound passion for knowledge and our admitted growing self-absorption.

In addition to these complicated schedules and strained relationships, many of us dealt with increasing financial pressures. As the saying goes, there are only so many hours in a day. Classes and studying inevitably took the place of some of the hours previously set aside for earning money. Like so many other families, Chip and I continued to struggle with the "how are we ever going to pay this bill" routine, and we became amazingly creative in finding ways to get by. To this day, my boys still remember their embarrassment at being on the free lunch program at school. But at the time, that type of assistance seemed like a lifesaver. It was sort of a nip-and-tuck balancing act. If you took a little off here, you could come up with that payment over there.

Eventually, though, I could no longer ignore the fact that I was going to have to take some time off from school in order to get a full time job. Our finances were weighing too heavily on all of us to be ignored. So even though it broke my heart, and Chip promised me it would only have to be for a year (a lifetime you say?!), I dropped out of Cal Poly and took a job running the front office of a custom photo lab. And every day I thought about school, and every day I couldn't wait to get back.

A year came and went, and while our finances had eased up a bit, they still weren't where we had hoped they would be. So I put off my return to school for a month, and then another month. But then after several additional months, I began to realize that things probably never were going to get to "that point" and it was time to come up with an alternative plan. There was simply no way I was *not* going back to school. So I contacted a good friend who had shown an interest in the position I held and convinced the owners of the lab to let us take a stab at job-sharing. They agreed, it worked, and I was back in school.

And when I went back to school this time—more determined than ever to achieve my goal—not only did I apply for student loans, but I also discovered, to my amazement, that there were scholarships specifically targeted at Returning Women. Apparently, society had decided by then that encouraging older women to return to school was a very honorable cause.

One available scholarship was offered by Soroptimist International, a well-respected professional women's organization. At the time, their scholarship was known as the T.A.P. award. (T.A.P. stands for the Training Awards Program.) The award is formally defined as "an initiative to help women who must enter the job market but lack the necessary skills or education." Informally, it is viewed as a scholarship for women who are struggling financially, have children dependent upon them, and who are trying to make something of themselves. Sounded good to me. Right up my alley, as a matter of fact. So I applied. And to my good fortune, I was chosen. There was only one catch, though. I had to give a speech, about twenty minutes long, about myself. Unless I was really uncomfortable with giving it. I said, no, I was sure I could think of something to say, and went about trying to figure out what exactly that would be.

I finally settled upon the fact that what I really needed to tell these women was how I got to be where I was. How did I get to be a thirty-year-old-woman with kids, financially destitute (well, okay, not quite, but close), going back to school. Just how did I end up qualifying for this award? I found that not only did I need to tell *them,* but I needed to tell myself.

So, after *another* round of self-evaluation (yes, we did a lot of that back then) and rehashing of events, I came up with a theory. I called it my Doris Day-Rock Hudson theory. You see, I started thinking back to when I was younger. I thought back to what made me happy. What were my dreams, and what did I expect out of life? What exactly, back then, did I think life was going to be like? And what came to mind were all those movies we so loved to watch. You know the ones I'm talking about . . .

Opening scene: Girl-next-door with *infectious* cheeriness lives alone and works at a job for either an interior decorator or fashion designer. Her friends keep telling her she needs to find a man to take care of her before it's too late. Along comes a *gorgeous* bundle of male hormones, usually with lots of money and a humorous male sidekick to keep things churned up. After their initial heart-pounding first glance, they clash head-on, she throws him out, until finally he utters those magic words: something like "And here I thought we were going to be married!" Girl-next-door visually melts; zoom in on glistening, sparkling eyes as she says, "Married? Did you say married?" Cut to a scene "nine months later" as husband proudly pushes baby carriage through a park under the smiling guidance of wife. Cut. The End. Happily Ever After.

Sighhhh . . . Wasn't that it? Wasn't that the way it was supposed to be?

It's not as if the messages spoon-fed to us in these films were new. Far from it. You can look back for centuries and the messages given to young women through literature and other forms of storytelling were essentially the same with an identical bottom line: In order to live happily ever after, you need to catch a husband. End of story, happy, happy, happy. And these stories and messages begin at such a tender young age. Cinderella, Sleeping Beauty, Snow White. Saved by the white knight on his beautiful white horse. "And they lived happily ever after."

Take a look at the novels of Jane Austen, which were written at the beginning of the nineteenth century and have recently found a whole new audience by way of movie remakes. While in the 1800s her messages clearly mirrored the stark economic reality of society, those same messages were carried forward by each generation and found their way into the romantic comedies of the 1960s. Modern translation: If you want to be happy for the rest of your life, do whatever it takes to nab a husband.

But I think that what made the romantic comedies so dear to us (and so influential upon our perception of reality) was the fact that we could relate to that girl-next-door. I mean, we *really could* be her. So even though, as little girls, we loved dressing up as princesses, pretending to be discovered by Prince Charming, we still knew deep down that we weren't princesses. For the most part, we were simply that girl-next-door, in the middle class neighborhood, hoping to lead a comfortable and happy life. You know, just like Doris Day.

In 1959 Doris Day first appeared with Rock Hudson in the romantic comedy *Pillow Talk.* And while she had starred with other popular leading men, such as Frank Sinatra, in earlier light-hearted films, there was a unique chemistry between her and Rock Hudson that "set the screen on fire." The era of romantic comedies took off, and women couldn't get enough of them. Doris Day starred in several additional comedies with Rock Hudson, and then successfully ventured out to face-off against other heart-throbs such as Cary Grant and James Garner.

Yet it was the combination of Doris Day and Rock Hudson that captured most of our hearts. They were simply so believable. They could really be us. We could really be them. We could see ourselves as that young woman working in one of those "fall back on" careers. Remember that strategy? Women felt that they needed to be trained in a profession—like teaching or interior decorating—so they would have something to "fall back on" in case they weren't able to catch a husband within an appropriate period of time. And as we bided our time in one of these jobs, we could truly see ourselves accidentally bumping into that all-American good-looking man, falling in love and living happily ever after. None of us seemed to question the fact that all of these stories, from Jane Austen to present day, ended with the marriage proposal and occasionally baby on the way. The stories seemed to tell us that the process ended there. You get to that point and Happily Ever After is guaranteed.

Let's face it, we didn't stand a chance. The main characters were beautiful, the music romantic, the story line bursting with humor and optimism. Forget the fact that it was just a movie. We wanted to believe that it was true and could happen to us. We came away from these movies believing that we didn't have to plan our lives, that we didn't have to make decisions about which direction we wanted to take. Most of us, if only subconsciously, assumed that we

would eventually marry and that Mr. Right (aka Prince Charming) would guide us, protect us, and make life wonderful. Just like in the movies.

But eventually, for so many women including myself, the Happily Ever After myth crumbled as reality turned out to be so different from the fairy tales. And in the ultimate ironic twist, along with all other lessons about the *real* reality, we even learned that Rock Hudson, that gorgeous hunk of all-American male, never would have been there for any of us. That, in reality, he chose a totally different path than we ever could have imagined. A lot of women's hearts broke during his tragic last days.

In all fairness, women were not the only victims of this storytelling misconception. Think about the fact that men were put in a position of having to fill the shoes of the likes of Cary Grant. Think about the expectations society put on them. Men were expected to be solely responsible for the financial well-being and overall happiness of their families. It seems that women clearly assumed that men went into marriage with some mysterious gene that made them automatically capable of satisfying these requirements. And while many of them were able to meet society's expectations, there were others who were simply unable to handle the often overwhelming responsibilities. The end result of their failure was usually a sense of disappointment and bitterness on the part of both spouses which remained as a barrier between them for the remainder of their lives together.

I also firmly believe that men ultimately lost out on the opportunity to spend their lives with someone who was striving for her own potential. Wives were often viewed more as dependents than as partners, and there was minimal understanding of the other spouse's role in the marriage. This built-in class system provided little chance for the sharing of experiences or an empathy for each other's challenges. I have to believe that sitting on top of a pedestal all by yourself can, at times, be a very lonely experience.

So that was my theory, way back then. And as the years have passed, and I have built a successful accounting practice working with women, and have listened to so many of their stories, I know, more than I ever did at that pivotal point in my life, how universally true that theory remains.

What about my own journey? I would love to tell you that Chip and I had one of those relationships that weathered all the highs and lows, but we didn't. We grew up together, and struggled together, but ultimately couldn't stay together. Unfortunately, the era of the Returning Women claimed its own victims. Many of us went into relationships saying, "This must be what I want." But as we grew as individuals, educated ourselves, and took long looks at what we truly wished for in life, a lot of us were forced to say, in all honesty, "I'm sorry, but this isn't really what I wanted." We had deceived our husbands as much as we had deceived ourselves. We discovered that no one else can make you happy if you are not happy with yourself.

Yet I do consider myself one of the more fortunate ones. Chip was, without a doubt, my most devoted cheerleader. To this day I know he is extremely proud of all that I have accomplished. And I firmly believe that we *all* need as many cheerleaders as we can get.

THE INVISIBLE WOMEN

As I grow older, I am increasingly amazed at the perpetual motion of time. Where, exactly, does it go so quickly? Over the last two decades we have watched—and at times participated—as women have made slow but steady advancements since their initial, awkward awakening. Statistics now abound relating to our repositioning in society, politics, and business, and our progress is graphically and continuously debated. Have we come too far, too fast (for some), or have we not come far enough, with no clear equity in sight (for others)?

The media and advertising industry have tried hard to keep up with our evolution, not wanting to lose an audience or miss influencing a sale. We have seen the commercial image of women transformed from the happy homemaker of the '50s and '60s into the perky, anything-goes Charlie Girl of the '70s, to the career woman of the '80s, then gradually eased into the successful, but older Baby Boomer of the '90s. If asked, most people would more than likely applaud the media and advertisers for such sensitivity to our growing independence and our hard-earned achievements. But I, for one, am concerned.

Have you ever thought about the magnitude of influence that the media has upon our perception of life? We rely so heavily upon this monstrous information-gathering machinery. We tend to accept what is fed to us by way of the daily newspaper and evening news broadcast, with a cascade of periodicals thrown in for good measure. We assume, after absorbing their stories, that we have a complete picture of the world as it really is. And here lies the problem: The media, as well as the advertising industry, has a very short attention span. It zeros in on the obvious—the most colorful, attention-grabbing stories and images. I am constantly amazed at the number of times a crisis in some foreign country has been reported, or an injustice exposed, only to disappear the next evening and never be addressed again. Does this mean that the small country in crisis has miraculously "fixed" the situation? Does this mean that those individuals hit with prejudice have suddenly received fair treatment? No, it simply means that the media has gone on to a more exciting story, one that will better capture the audience's attention. So these stories and images quietly slip out of our minds and are replaced by other subsequent, pre-selected images. Images that claim to define the world around us.

My experiences as a Returning Woman came at a time when the media embraced, and gallantly applauded, late-blooming women. We were a novel bunch back then, and society openly encouraged us to return to school to "make something of ourselves." We were one of the media's very "in" little causes at the time. Our efforts flowed easily into the documented transition of housewives to economic partners. And for this I have to honestly say, "Thank you. It helped." There is nothing quite like a rooting section and a few good cheerleaders to give you that extra push towards your goals.

But those days are long gone, and everyone clearly knows that all women in our society have "figured it out" by now. The lessons have been learned; we think for ourselves and choose to be independent. Right? Every news program you turn to these days, every newspaper edition or monthly periodical you read, has a story about women turning 50, or women turning 60, and how they are slowing down after that successful career, how they are transitioning, yet blossoming, from a fast track existence to a slower paced, more pensive one. So this is who we all must be. The stereotype is so clean and well-defined. It gives absolutely no indication that a silent sorority of women has been inconspicuously left behind. That a surprisingly large segment of our society very quietly, and ever-so politely, continues on as usual, unnoticed and unchanged by all the hoopla over women's independence. They have no formal rooting section, and most of their cheerleaders have moved on to more visible causes. But they do exist, and I need to tell you that I see these women daily.

I see the women who chose "traditional" relationships early in life and were settled into a comfortable routine when others decided to fight for independence and voice. I see the women who shared responsibilities with their husbands the old-fashioned way because that is how they were raised and that is what they believed in. I see the women who were told, "Don't worry about a thing. I'll take care of you." And I see the women whose husbands have now died or left them, and these women haven't a clue what to do next.

That's right. They're out there. And here you thought you were the only one.

It is easier for society to presume that everyone is "okay," that all women are in control and handling life's little ups and downs just fine, thank you very much. Less guilt and anxiety are involved. Yet this presumption is, in fact, one of the very barriers that keeps so many women (like yourself) from standing up and saying, "Excuse me, but I need some help. I haven't quite figured this out yet." There aren't many of us who enjoy drawing attention to ourselves by admitting that we don't quite measure up to someone else's expectations. It is so much easier to quietly carry on as usual, with minimal confidence, not asking any obvious questions, and hoping that nobody will notice. Well, guess what? I'VE NOTICED. And it's time we do something about it!

To say that you are not alone is a *major* understatement. Do you have any idea just how "not alone" you are? According to the U.S. Census Bureau, there are almost 200 million adults living in the United States and over half of these adults are women. Out of this huge population of adult women, 22 million of them are either divorced or widowed. As our population ages, and women continue to outlive their husbands, these figures are expected to increase significantly. Right now, over half of all older women (65 years and up) are either divorced or widowed.

All of these women are trying to figure out how to deal with the world on their own. And the majority of these unwitting sorority members share the following traits:

- They are terrified of facing the world alone.
- They think of themselves as being stupid or just not very bright.
- They view themselves as being inferior to most of the people they interact with.
- They place no importance on what they personally know, yet place a great deal of importance on the knowledge of others.
- They have no confidence in decisions that they have to make on their own.
- And finally, they do not feel that they have any control

over their own lives. They view themselves as helpless, as merely victims of what takes place in the world around them.

Now if, in all honesty, you can relate to how these women feel, you should be proud of the fact that you are able to see this in yourself. Acknowledging a problem is the first step to solving it. Don't ever put yourself down for who you are or where you've been. Remember, you are the product of a society that raised you with idealistic dreams and images and then didn't bother to prepare you for one of the more probable story lines. Like so many others, you are merely suffering from what I like to call the Beyond Happily Ever After Syndrome.

The good news, though, is that it is NEVER too late to make changes in your life for the better. We are all so much stronger than we give ourselves credit for. Would you like to feel in control of your life? Would you like to feel more confident around other people? Would you like to get rid of the fear of making decisions on your own, get rid of the insecurities in your day-to-day living? You can. You really can survive beyond Happily Ever After.

COME JOIN US!

Admittedly, there is a percentage of women in our society who, from the very beginning, understood that they had the ability to control their own lives and destiny. They had the inner strength and confidence to defy society's stereotypes and expectations. All the rest of us, at one stage in our lives or another, have had to figure it out as we went along. Some of us figured it out early in life, while others of us figured it out later when things became a little more complicated. But the point is that to one degree or another we have all "been there." The only difference between us has been in the timing. You are no different than those women who got there before you. Those women you see on the street or in offices or at parties who seem to have it all together. It's merely in the timing. And now it is *your* turn.

I personally find strength in knowing that we all share in this learning process. Even some of the most powerful women in our society have "been there" and have had to struggle in their own way to get to the position in life that they are in today. Take a look at Katharine Graham, longtime publisher of the *Washington Post* and one of the most admired and feared women in America. She recently received a Pulitzer Prize for her autobiography *Personal History* in which she discusses how she let life just happen to her. She states that "Rather than creating my own way, what I was trying to do all the time was figure out how to adjust to whatever life I found." In reference to her husband she states that ". . . always, it was he who decided and I who responded." It wasn't until after her husband's emotional decline and ultimate suicide that she was forced to find her own inner strength and then went on to control the course of her own life. Millions of us have survived and even thrived. You can do it, too.

There is a catch, though, that I need to mention. You have got to "want it bad." Not just "kind of." Not just "maybe I'll give it a half-hearted try." You have got to realize and accept, deep down, in your heart, that no one else can change your life but you. You have got to accept the fact that you are ultimately the only one responsible for who you are and where you're going. No one else can do it for you. Remember: "You can change those areas of your life with which you are less than pleased, but you must take responsibility for your being."

So, are you willing to give it a whole-hearted try? I truly hope so, because the rewards are simply beyond belief. The world will open up to you with new opportunities that you have never considered before. You won't be afraid to get out of bed in the morning, to meet new people or try new challenges. Instead, you'll feel like a brand new person, full of potential and full of confidence. And you will be able to start telling yourself: "I can do this!"

Part II of this book shows you *how* to survive and thrive. The steps are not hard; we keep it simple. So tell yourself you can do it, and dig in!

COME JOIN US!

Part II

Survival Training

PRE-CONDITIONING—THE DON'T RULES

Have you ever noticed that at times it can be easier, and often more precise, to describe something by focusing on what it is NOT—versus what it IS? For example, when people ask me to describe the type of clients I prefer to work with, it is so much easier to simply describe the group of people I *least* like to work with—that group being "middle-aged males in business for themselves with pension plans." (They always need to prove that they know so much more than I do!) This process of elimination in turn emphasizes all of those people I *do* enjoy working with: young people on their way up, retired people, and women in all phases of life. Less ego seems to be involved.

Another example—people who enjoy the fine arts may at times discover that an art form is best described by the negative space around it. Or, on a more basic level, think about how often grandparents emphasize the importance of good posture by demanding, "Don't slouch!" Sometimes, pointing out the negative can be the most powerful approach to emphasizing the positive.

Yet, admittedly, when it came time to put down on paper a set of general guidelines that would provide a solid starting point, or framework, for this new adventure of gaining control of your life, I was frustrated to find that I kept going back to concepts that were in the form of what *not* to do. I was somewhat perplexed and felt that this approach was not appropriate for a book that is meant to encourage. I mean, a whole chapter on "negatives" did not seem to be very uplifting! But the more I thought about it, the more I began to realize that this approach is exactly what is needed. I began to realize that what we are actually doing here is first eliminating the old negative habits and reactions that have become an integral part of your relationship with the rest of the world. Old habits and reactions that have allowed other people and events to control the course of your life. By eliminating these patterns, you can turn the tables on your position in life and gain control yourself. And only then will you be able to start visualizing and working towards all those new, wonderful things you will gradually realize you can do. So let's start eliminating. Here we go—the Don't Rules:

Rule #1: Don't feel sorry for yourself.

Life is *not* fair. Get over it. You are who you are, you are where you are, and you *cannot* change the path that got you there. We all have areas of our own personal history that we would give anything to rewrite. We can't. And feeling sorry for ourselves because of events that took place in our past is a waste of valuable time. Self-pity is destructive. Self-pity is paralyzing. You will not get anywhere in life if you feel sorry for yourself. It is truly that simple.

Let's talk about crying. Crying is, without a doubt, the most common physical reaction to self-pity among women. When something unpleasant happens, when we feel a situation has turned against us, and our response to that situation is a feeling of helplessness and being out-of-control, tears well up in our eyes and flow down our cheeks. And let's be honest here—crying feels good. It is an intense emotional release that occurs when we don't know what else to do. How do I know this?

Because I clearly remember my own hours of sitting in solitude, where no one else could see me, crying my heart out and not knowing what to do next.

But the problem with crying is that it takes so much energy and is so non-productive. After a "good cry," you're emotionally spent and you have no energy left to do anything else. Like solve your problems. Like take control of the situation. Or like get angry. Yes—that's what I said—get angry. If you can replace self-pity with any other emotion, anger is by far your best bet. You'd be amazed at what you can do if you allow yourself to get "ticked off." No doubt about it, anger can be *extremely* motivating.

So next time the tears start welling up, tell yourself, damn it, I'm not going to react this way anymore. I'm not going to just sit here and let things happen to me. I am not going to waste my time crying. I'm going to do something about this. And you know what? Once you break that habit of crying, you're going to find that you have a ton of energy for productive, positive action.

Do I cry anymore? Sure I do. But I save it for the really important stuff.

Rule #2: Don't dwell on or live in the past.

This rule is so closely tied to Rule #1 that I probably should have called it Rule #1A. This rule is about getting on with your life, about letting go of that event, or series of events, that left you in your current less-than-comfortable position. The death of your husband, that string of "bad luck," that messy divorce. *Especially* that messy divorce. Let it go. I repeat—let it go. I know this may come as a shock to you, but nobody really wants to hear about it. You see, the past gets in the way of focusing on the future. And the future is what counts. Go back to Rule #1. You can't change the past, and wallowing in it prevents you from making a bright new future. When you continually burden other people with your story, trying to hang on to that past, they will more than likely respond by doing two things: first, they will feel sorry for you. And then, they will gradually tune out.

Several years back, my new husband, Larry, ran into an old friend he hadn't seen for some time and she invited the two of us over for dinner. She had been married to a wealthy, older businessman for several years; they had adopted two small children, and then the marriage fell apart and they divorced. We had heard that the divorce had been messy, a real down-and-dirty battle to be exact, but that it was now finalized. We looked forward to a pleasant evening with Kelly and her new gentleman friend, drinking good wine, eating good food, and talking about their new life together.

What we got, instead, was a blow-by-blow account of the whole divorce, accompanied by a massive album containing letters and documents outlining the most horrific accusations and details, all of which we would rather not have known. It became clear to us that Kelly's primary reason for having us over was not to enjoy the present, but to have an attentive audience that would allow her to relive, over and over, her obsessive past.

Needless to say, we did not pursue any subsequent get-togethers. We have heard reports from mutual acquaintances that Kelly and her ex-husband continued to battle on, even after the divorce, with the children caught in the middle, using up all of their resources and energy. He ultimately filed for bankruptcy, in a blatant and successful maneuver to keep her from acquiring any further financial resources from him. She ended up with next to nothing, living alone.

Such a waste of time and energy. You can't change the past and you can't live in it. Get on with life.

Rule #3: Don't try to be 20 years old again, and don't try to compete with those who currently are that age.

There is something very powerful about maturity. It can be sexy; it can be a class act. Accept where you are in life and use your age and experience to your advantage, with dignity and a sense of humor. If you need role models, they are very easy to find. Audrey Hepburn was without a doubt my favorite. What style and composure. Then there is Katharine Hepburn, Lauren Bacall, Jacqueline Bissett . . . The list is extensive. They don't try to be younger than they are.

Instead, they have grace and class and power. They know that they have something that no young thing can claim: self-confidence acquired through years of experience.

I find that the people I most enjoy being around are those who are obviously comfortable with who they are. They like themselves, they don't take themselves too seriously, and they're not trying to be somebody else. Trust me, it shows. Be yourself.

Rule #4: Don't keep coming up with reasons and excuses why you just can't quite get control of your life, like right now, this very minute, you know, it's all very complicated and all that and you just can't find the time because you've been left with this mess, and then there is that other problem . . .

I know, I know. This statement does run on a bit, but that is exactly what people with excuses do. Remember—"You can change those areas of your life with which you are less than pleased, but *you must take responsibility for your being.*" Stop blaming events, stop blaming other people. It's your life. Take control of it. Now.

Anecdotes *abound* on this Rule. Letting go of excuses and taking responsibility for your life is one of the toughest hurdles to overcome. My client, Gail, comes to mind first. She's a realtor who filed for bankruptcy the year before I met her due to the fact, she said, that her ex-husband ran up all their joint credit cards. She then had a few good years of income as a self-employed individual, but ended up owing the IRS a bunch of money for taxes that she couldn't pay. This time it was because her mother was ill, her car needed to be replaced, and her boyfriend wanted her to start contributing to the mortgage payments on the huge house they lived in. So we eventually resolved that problem, she settled into a very lucrative position selling timeshares, and I assumed all was finally well because her employer was withholding taxes from her paycheck. Wrong. Some co-workers told her that she should claim all these extra exemptions so that her withholding would be less, and therefore her take-home pay would be more. And, gosh, when she told me over the phone, towards the end of the year, what her withholding was, so that we could make sure there was enough to cover her projected taxes in April, she just happened to read the wrong figure. So there she was, again, April 15th, owing the IRS about $23,000, and it wasn't her fault. Isn't life unfair!

Again, it's your life. Stop making excuses and take control of it. Now.

Rule #5: Don't accept the role of a featherbrain or ditz. (Ditz \dit-s\ n: uneducated, scatterbrained female. Unable to comprehend three syllable words. Most commonly associated with well-endowed bleached blondes. Adj: ditzy.)

Don't fool yourself, or others, into believing that you are not smart enough to make decisions on your own, or not smart enough to process and retain information given to you by others. While some women admittedly enjoy playing this role because it is simply easier to act helpless and in need of guidance, there are many, many women who assume this position because this is exactly what our society has programmed them to do. They were both raised and married in an environment which was filled with comments such as the following:

"Don't worry your pretty little head about it."
"I'll take care of this for you. It's very confusing."
"Trust me. I'll handle everything."

"It's really too complicated for you to understand."
"It's simply a bunch of complex legal jargon."
"Don't worry about it; I've read it. Just sign here."

If not given much thought, statements like the above have the potential for being very comforting. They can make you feel protected and taken care of. They can make you feel loved and watched over. But, unfortunately, they can also provide you with a false sense of security, in addition to a built-in lack of self-confidence.

A few weeks ago I had the most inspiring phone conversation with a new client referred to me by a female attorney. Her name is Jill. When we spoke, Jill was gracious and eloquent in telling me her story, but clearly very angry. She told me about how her husband had always taken such good care of her during their lengthy marriage. He had handled all of their financial and legal matters, made all of the important decisions, and she, in turn, had taken care of their home. He constantly told her that he was "protecting her from the cold, harsh world." He passed away about a year before our conversation.

In Jill's words, she quickly discovered that "he had not done me any favors." She stated that being left to deal with the world on her own was like "being thrown into a lake without knowing how to swim." She literally didn't know how to write a check. There were all kinds of decisions that needed to be made and she didn't know how to make them. She initially relied upon associates of her late husband to help her unravel her financial matters, only to discover later that many of them took advantage of her for their own financial gain. But gradually, like so many other women before her, she began to realize that she had the ability to learn, that she had the ability to make her own decisions and find advisors whom she personally related to and trusted. And she was going to make it on her own, by God. What a great lady. I have yet to meet her, but I can't wait.

Now, there is no question that letting go of the need-to-be-taken-care-of role is hard to do. Because if you have been told all your life that "it's just too complicated for you to understand, so don't worry your little head about it," you are bound to believe that you do not have the ability to make decisions on your own. But the reality is that you DO have the ability to make decisions and gain control of your life if you want to badly enough. Repeat after me: "I am NOT stupid. I CAN understand the information that is being given to me." And every time you get into a position where someone else is trying to do the thinking for you, or someone is offering information on a subject that you haven't had to handle before, repeat it again. No, you are not stupid. You can understand the information that is being explained to you. Repeat it often enough, and pretty soon you will start believing it.

It is all a matter of focusing, asking the right questions and believing in yourself. Playing the part of the ditz is an easy way out that allows other people to take advantage of you. And, besides, it just isn't fashionable any more.

Rule #6: Don't allow yourself to be intimidated by people who have more education or business experience than you do, whether it is someone you meet at a cocktail party, or a professional you rely on for advice.

What you need to realize is that all of these people, with their higher education or vast business experience, simply happen to have had a head start in gathering useful information—that's all. They are not smarter than you; they are not better than you. They just got a head start. (Go back to Rule #5: *You are not stupid. Do not accept the role of featherbrain or ditz.*)

The bottom line is that all people, no matter what their dress, what their education or title, are simply, deep down, just human beings like you and me. No better, no worse. Do not allow yourself to believe otherwise.

This rule is extremely important in order to get the most out of life and relationships. If you act inferior or apologetic around another individual, you immediately put restrictions on your conversation and your relationship. People are much more interested in talking to someone who clearly believes in her own potential and is willing to learn, rather than talking to someone who projects an image that says, " I'm not very smart and I probably won't understand a thing you tell me."

So don't be afraid to interact with people you find interesting or people you feel may hold more knowledge or experience than you do. Never apologize for who you are or where you've been.

Rule #7: Don't make the assumption that these same people with more education or business experience or titles, these people in "power" positions, are in control of their own lives.

Success and control are not necessarily synonymous, just as success and happiness are not synonymous. Far from it. Some of the most privately out-of-control people I know are those who have a solid in-control professional reputation. These individuals have simply learned how to wear a good "in-control" facade. Trust me, it's all in the posture.

Think back to some of the news headlines we've read: A well-respected judge turns out to have a fatal attraction relationship with a well-known socialite. Another highly visible public figure is found to prefer women's clothing and garter belts in his private life. (Is it relevant that the ones that immediately come to mind are all men?!) Don't assume everyone else is in control.

There is a mind game used in college speech classes that might be helpful for putting Rules #6 and #7 into practice. In order to help students feel less intimidated when speaking to a large crowd, they are often encouraged to imagine that everyone in the audience is sitting there without any clothes on. Brings the intimidation factor down a few notches, doesn't it? Try this next time you're meeting someone whose position, or mere presence, intimidates you. Could be fun. But try to keep a straight face.

Rule #8: Don't be afraid to try.

Women, in general, have an aversion to risk. If there is even the slightest chance that we might fail at something, most of us will choose to simply not even try. We would rather look the other way and hope that the situation or opportunity will quietly disappear. Men, on the other hand, actually *brag* about the times in which they have tried and failed. Think about the infinite number of huge fish that got away. And how many times have you been at a cocktail party and overheard a man talking about that million dollar life insurance policy he almost sold, but . . . or that multi-million dollar deal that would have gone through if only . . . So why do men do that?

My own personal theory is that men (again, in general) want the world to know that they are alive, that they are, in fact, living life to the fullest. They are taking chances and they are sometimes winning—sometimes not. But no matter which outcome, they have done it with gusto. You see, most of them understand that if you are always playing it safe, you're never going to experience life at its best. You are never going to experience some of life's most wonderful highs, because you will forever be trying to avoid any of life's possible lows. So what you end up with is safe, but dull.

Do not be afraid to take a chance. Do not be afraid to really experience what it feels like to be alive. You'll find that the rest of us are right there with you, learning to take chances, learning to get our knees dirty on occasion. What you will also discover, if you take that chance, is that succeeding at something—something which may have intimidated you in the past—will make you feel that you can do anything. It will make you smile. It will make you look in the mirror and say "Yes!" It will make you feel that you can conquer the world. And once you have succeeded at that first something new, you will also discover that occasionally falling on your face does not mean the end of the world. It just means you have a few new "war stories" to tell at the next cocktail party. So go for it. Start experiencing life.

Rule #9: Don't take life too seriously.

No, life is not fair, and yes, shit happens. We can't change any of that. What we can change is how we react to it. Think back, again, to how you viewed life as a child. Think back to the funny moments of life, the flower fields or sunsets that took your breath away. Think back to the most outrageous joke you ever heard, which probably had a trace of life's darker side woven into it, making the punch line all that more meaningful. You can either allow the harshness of life to take over your existence, or you can allow the humor and beauty of life to take center stage.

I, personally, am one of those people who tends to view a glass as half full versus half empty. I am also one of those people who tends to find a little bit of humor in just about any aspect or situation of life, sometimes to the great annoyance of my children. Yet that humor is what has gotten me through some really rough times, and that humor is what allows me to reach out to other women who are afraid of what life has to offer them.

Don't take life too seriously. Look for the joy; look for the humor. It's a big, beautiful, funny world out there if you allow it to be.

Rule #10: Finally, whatever you do, DO NOT keep waiting for Rock Hudson. Because he's not going to show.

The idea of a knight in shining armor coming to the rescue, or Cary Grant arriving at your doorstep to make the big, bad world go away, just doesn't work anymore. To be honest with you, I don't think it really ever did. A false sense of security can be a dangerous thing. Take responsibility for your own being.

Negative habits are extremely hard to break, especially when they have been reinforced repeatedly over 40 or 50 years. It is one thing for me to write these rules down on nice, clean white sheets of paper and then simply say, "Don't do this anymore." But it is an excruciatingly harder process to change these ingrained habits in real life. Don't for one minute think that it is going to be easy, because you will be sorely disappointed.

The good news, though, is that you CAN do it. I've done it, millions of other women have done it, and it FEELS GREAT. Every time you catch yourself doing one of the "Don'ts," just tell yourself to knock it off! Get angry! You're not going to get anywhere if you continue to react that way. If you keep reminding yourself to change these old knee-jerk reactions, then slowly, very slowly, your *new* reactions will become your habits.

Taking control of your life is powerful. No longer being a victim gives you strength. If you get nothing more out of this book than simply applying the Don't Rules to your life, you will have taken some very big steps.

The Don't Rules

Rule #1: Don't feel sorry for yourself.

Rule #2: Don't dwell on or live in the past.

Rule #3: Don't try to be 20 years old again, and don't try to compete with those who currently are that age.

Rule #4: Don't keep coming up with reasons and excuses why you just can't quite get control of your life.

Rule #5: Don't accept the role of featherbrain or ditz.

Rule #6: Don't allow yourself to be intimidated by people who have more education or business experience than you do.

Rule #7: Don't make the assumption that these same people with more education or business experience or titles are in control of their own lives.

Rule #8: Don't be afraid to try.

Rule #9: Don't take life too seriously.

Rule #10: Don't keep waiting for Rock Hudson. Because he's not going to show.

THE POWER OF INFORMATION AND WHERE TO FIND IT

Now that we've set aside our negative baggage, let's start focusing on some good, positive re-direction.

What is one of the first things you have to figure out when you start a new project? You need to determine what type of tools are required. And yes, what you're doing here is starting a project—one of the most important projects of your life. You have a goal—this confidence-building, this regaining control—and with the right tools you're going to be able to create a whole new approach to life that will allow you to achieve this goal.

Luckily, there are only two essential tools that you will need to learn how to use and become comfortable with: *Information* and *money.* Simple, direct and powerful tools that can take you anywhere you want to go. Because contrary to the song, love does not make the world go 'round. Information and money do. Let's take a look at information first, and I'll show you why.

What exactly is information? It is nothing more than an accumulation of facts and data that allow you to better understand and react to the world around you. Information prepares you for the outcome or consequences of a set of events or circumstances. Information helps you to more confidently make decisions with a better understanding of the outcome of those decisions. In other words, acquiring the right information can assist you in controlling the course of your life.

Think about the importance of information in your everyday world. Let's look at something as simple as washing clothes. You have a pile of clothes on the floor. You pull out the red socks and green shirt and set them aside so that you can wash the whites by themselves. When the load is finished, you hang up two all-cotton shirts to dry instead of putting them in the dryer.

Facts, decisions, consequences. You know that the red socks and green shirt will bleed and turn the white clothes pink and lime if you wash them together. You know that the cotton shirts will shrink if you put them in the dryer. You may have learned this information from your mother, from direct experience (I personally learned that boys do *not* appreciate pink underwear), or from reading labels. But no matter where you acquired it, you used that information to make decisions in order to obtain the desired consequences.

The same basic chain of events occurs in the world outside your home. You acquire facts to support your decisions, which in turn lead you towards the desired consequences. It's that simple.

You need to think of decision making as a process similar to putting together a jigsaw puzzle. If you don't have all the pieces of a puzzle, there is no way you can finish putting it together. Data and facts, similarly, are the pieces of your puzzle when making a decision. If you do not have adequate information needed to form a clear "picture" of the situation, there is no way that you can make a decision with any kind of confidence as to what the outcome will be.

Unfortunately, when it comes to making decisions in unfamiliar territory, a lot of people tend to overlook the fact that they simply need to gather enough information on the existing circumstances in order to make an intelligent decision. They instead assume that they are basically not intelligent enough to make that type of decision. When, in reality, all they probably need are just a few more facts.

As a perfect example, junior staff members in legal and accounting firms learn this lesson, like most of us, the hard way. You're new to the job, you're terrified of the senior partners, you have absolutely no confidence in yourself, and you're given a project that you can't quite tie together. In addition, you're too intimidated to ask questions for fear of looking stupid. (Want to hear some really intense self-degradation? Just look inside the mind of a junior staffer!) Yet, somehow, most of these new "staffers" manage to survive the first project, and then the next one, and then the next. What they begin to realize is that they are not stupid, that they do have the basic skills to figure out what they're supposed to be doing, and if they're unable to complete a specific project it is probably because someone, either their boss or possibly the client, has not given them enough information.

The key to *all* decision making, the key to being in control of *any* situation, is making sure you acquire adequate information. You know that stockbroker you work with, or the CPA who does your taxes? Think back to Rule #6: *They are no smarter than you, or better than you.* They have simply acquired a few more facts than you have relating to their area of expertise. That's all. And you are just as capable as anyone else on this earth of gathering information necessary to make decisions that will direct the course of your life. You ARE capable.

Unfortunately, one of the biggest misconceptions held by people who lack confidence in themselves is that the only real way to acquire important information is through a formal education. (i.e., go back to college and get a four-year degree.) And if you don't have one of those four-year degrees, you must not be as smart as that person who does have one. What needs to be understood here is that information and formal education are not the same thing. Formal education is merely one of many ways to obtain information.

The problem with getting a formal education is that you're usually required to subject yourself to a lengthy series of classes that are intended to turn you into a "well-rounded" human being. Not only do you take courses that relate to your particular field of interest, but you must also take a broad range of courses in subjects that fall into that "well-rounded" category. For instance, you may be required to dissect frogs in a biology class even though your area of interest is finance. Or you may be required to suffer through a mathematical statistics class (one of my least favorite) even though your focus is on art history.

But if you eventually do survive those years of doggedly passing and checking off every one of the required courses (most of which will never be called upon in real life), you'll receive a piece of paper that tells the world that you are an "educated person" and can now pursue a particular profession or, if nothing more, at least sound intelligent at cocktail parties. (That's right. Remember that guy you met at the cocktail party in Rule #6? *This* is how he got so cocky.)

There is no question that a formal education can provide a wonderful boost of confidence, as well as a required stepping-stone for many careers. And, if you let it, it will allow you to see the whole world with expanded horizons. My own personal achievement of earning a four-year degree still ranks as one of the most important accomplishments and hurdles of my life. It convinced me that I could achieve *anything* if I wanted to badly enough. But a formal education is also a very time-consuming goal, and it does not necessarily provide you with practical information relevant to your life and your current situation.

What you need right now is quality versus quantity. What you need is a unique package of information that is custom-made to help you make decisions NOW. (Don't you just love it when someone tells you that instant gratification can be a *good* thing!) If you really want to pursue a formal degree, I encourage you to do so. But view it as a long-term project. Right now what you need is that instant gratification stuff.

Fortunately for all of us, there are numerous alternate ways to obtain information. These techniques are not new. They are things you probably do already, but just don't do often enough or efficiently enough. They require a little confidence, a little creativity, and a lot of determination. Let's look at a few.

Ask Questions

Think back to when your kids were little or, for that matter, when you were little. What is the one thing that little kids do incessantly? They ask questions. Constantly, annoyingly, endlessly. Mommy, how come the water is so cold? Daddy, what are you fixing? Mommy, where does the sun go at night? Mommy, why does Grandma always wear that silly hat? Why, Mommy, why?

Asking questions is the most fundamental form of information-gathering we have available. It is the first technique we instinctively use. But unfortunately, while society instills in us the belief that knowledge, or the accumulation of information, is power, we conversely grow up to believe that *lack* of knowledge is therefore a sign of weakness. Similar to those junior staffers at the accounting firms, we become too intimidated to ask questions for fear of being ridiculed. No one wants to look ignorant. And because of this fear of being ridiculed, we shut down a highly valuable means of educating ourselves.

You may not want to admit that you're afraid to ask questions, but believe me, at one time or another almost everyone is intimidated. One of the most common phrases I hear from women I work with is, "I have a stupid question to ask you." Please understand what I am about to tell you: THERE IS NO SUCH THING AS A STUPID QUESTION. Think about it. What is so stupid about gathering information so that you can make an intelligent decision? What is so stupid about your determination to educate yourself? Keep in mind that the only difference between you and the people you are questioning is the fact that they just happened to have acquired pieces of information before you did. That definitely does not make them any better than you. It merely means, again, that they got a head start. That's all.

And while the process of asking questions may sound simple enough, there are certain guidelines you should follow in order to get the most benefit from your efforts:

#1: Direct your questions to people who are in the position to know the answer.

Translation: Do not ask your auto mechanic whether you should sell your IBM stock. Do not ask your next-door neighbor which health insurance policy you should buy. And do not (this, of course, is my personal favorite) ask your tennis partner if you need to file a tax return.

Everyone loves to give advice. Pure and simple. In every neighborhood, every party, every gathering of two or more people, there is someone who is an informal expert on every subject you can think of. And he will gladly tell you how to run you life, fix your car, invest your money.

The trap we fall into is that it is less intimidating to ask advice of a "non-expert," a regular guy, than to approach someone who is experienced in the area in question and who might, you fear, think your question is stupid.

So what is wrong with getting your information from this regular guy? Two things. First, his jigsaw puzzle is more than likely different from your jigsaw puzzle. Everyone's circumstances in life are unique. Very few people lead identical lives. So while this regular guy may have pulled together enough facts, or pieces of the puzzle, to make decisions that work in *his* life, the pieces of *your* puzzle will more than likely be different from his, warranting different decisions and different consequences. It is important that you ask advice from people who have dealt with a wide range of situations and fact-combinations, and who know how to head you in the right direction based upon *your* particular circumstances.

The second problem with getting your information from the regular guy is that information passed on at parties, over fences, or on tennis courts is usually what I call "popular" information. It is information that people *want* to hear, that people *want* to believe is true. It is not necessarily correct information; it is just popular information. The old saying that people hear what they want to hear is unfortunately true. Popular information is the type of information that is printed in LARGE LETTERS in advertisements meant to grab people's attention. The most recent example I can think of was a bank promotion stating something like: "Get a free trip to Hawaii simply by opening up a checking account!!" Sounds great! But what is missing in popular information is the fine print—those additional facts that give you a more complete picture—and usually take you back to reality. In this case, I learned that the ticket you received was so restricted that you basically had to fly stand-by and, in addition, you had to agree to buy an exorbitantly-priced week in a given hotel that more than negated the savings you received on that "free" ticket.

And no one can ever really pinpoint the original source of popular information. John heard it from Sue who heard it from Uncle Bob who may have heard it from his lawyer. Who lives in another state. Who doesn't know a thing about California law. And you live in California. Facts, unfortunately, have a way of becoming distorted when passed from one regular guy to another. So go to a direct source. Ask questions of people who can back up their answers with facts.

#2: Do not apologize for asking a question.

As I said before, why should you apologize for wanting to educate yourself? Besides, I fully believe that one of the primary responsibilities of people in business is to answer questions and educate the people they are working with. It is very easy to be intimidated into forgetting a very simple fact: The professionals you pay to assist you, whether they be doctors, lawyers or accountants, are supposed to be working for *you*. They are there to offer you a service. You do not go to see them simply to make them feel more important. They are there to provide you with information. So ask away.

#3: Listen.

Asking a question is a waste of everyone's time if you do not listen to the answer. The only time a question borders on being stupid is if you have already asked the question and didn't pay attention to the answer. This is where Rule #5 comes in: *Don't play the part of a ditz.* Give yourself some credit. Focus. Pay attention to what the person has to say and give yourself time to think about what he said. Write it down if necessary. Then, if for some reason the answer he gave you still isn't clear, go ahead and ask the person to rephrase or clarify the answer. Then listen again.

Finally, do not be selective in your listening, or you will end up turning good information into popular information. Take the bad news with the good. Be honest with yourself. Otherwise you will only be deceiving yourself when making decisions based upon that filtered information, and you will ultimately be disappointed in the consequences.

Read

Reading is magical. Reading can be exciting and powerful and ever so liberating. Reading can open up your whole world to endless possibilities. And no other activity is more flexible or has more potential for gathering information relevant to your personal existence and the world around you.

Think about it. You can pick up a book, magazine or newspaper and read it any time, anywhere. In an airport, on the beach, in your bedroom. At 2:00 in the afternoon or 2:00 in the morning. You can be wearing sweats, no make up, curled up on the couch or soaking in the tub, reading at the same time. (Where are you reading this book right now?)

Reading is the *ultimate* in self-reliance. You don't have to make an appointment, make a phone call, or be intimidated by another person's response to your questions. You can underline, copy, read as little as you want, or as much as you want. And if you don't get something the first time, you can reread it as many times as you like. Once you get a taste for it, reading is downright addictive.

If bookstores are not where you normally hang out, it's time to change your habits. Set aside some free time (or *make* some time—it's that important), locate the nearest bookstore, and take a slow stroll through the nonfiction aisles. Notice how the books are organized by subject, and wander through areas that draw your attention. Pull out a book or two that catch your eye and flip through them to get a feel for the writing style of the author and content of the book. Don't be in a hurry. Enjoy the process. Then, if a particular book eventually piques your curiosity about what it has to offer you, if you like the way it appears to be written, and it simply feels good in your hands (don't laugh—to me this is very important), you probably have the beginning of a beautiful friendship.

Keep in mind that the same experience can be had at your local library, depending, of course, upon the expanse of its book inventory. Libraries are a good "cheap read." For a very reasonable fee you can get a library card and then read for free to your heart's content. (Unless, of course, you have a bad habit of not returning books on time.) And the library staff can be invaluably helpful. A perfect source to direct your questions to. I must confess, though, that I have a real thing about owning books that I read or fall in love with. I simply have to have books around me. Seeing a book on the shelf, or merely knowing that it is there, brings back to mind the knowledge or good feelings I may have drawn from it.

The subjects you can learn about through reading are literally endless. And there is currently a growing trend towards publishing "user-friendly" books on once-difficult to understand (or boring) subjects. The series of "Dummies" books has been a smashing commercial success and includes, among others, *Investing for Dummies, Computers for Dummies,* even *Sex for Dummies.* (Honest.) The publishing world has finally figured out that people of average intelligence do not want to be talked down to. They have finally figured out that it is possible to address just about any subject in terms that most people can understand. So no longer do you have to wade through a ten-pound, three-inch, hardbound edition entitled something like *The Comprehensive Journal of Trading Intangible Property Over the Past 100 Years* in order to gain a general understanding of the stock market.

There is a wonderfully decadent aspect about reading and purchasing books that most professionals, and definitely most writers, will not openly acknowledge. And that is . . . you don't *have* to read the whole book! Gasp! I know, I know. That goes against *everything* that you were ever taught in school and had reinforced by your parents in terms of frugality. You must clean your plate, you must finish the whole book, etc., etc. But really, think about it. In our increasingly high-tech, high-complex society, there is simply too much information on any one subject for any one person to assimilate. Professionals may not admit it, but there is no way that a lawyer, for example, can memorize all facts and data relevant to his profession or even his area of specialization. And there really is no need to. All professionals have reference libraries, which are nothing more than volumes of information pertaining to subjects they deal with in their field. There is no reason why *you* shouldn't have such a library, no matter how big or small.

Reference libraries simply store quantities of information, on a variety of subjects, accessible to you when you need them. These books are not necessarily meant to be read from beginning to end. A lot of information is too intense to be absorbed all at once, or even in numerous sittings. Then there are the subjects that you know are relevant to decisions you will need to make in your life but, quite honestly, they put you to sleep. I personally can think of one or two subjects that cause *my* eyes to glaze over every time I try to read more than a few pages at a time on that particular topic. No problem. I simply keep books on these subjects in my reference library. I have not read most of them all the way through, but I know where to find them when I need to look something up.

If you're intrigued enough by a subject to read a whole book on it, cover to cover—great. More power to you. But, on the other hand, do not put off buying a book on a subject relevant to your life simply because you cannot envision curling up with it and a warm cup of cocoa for an exciting evening. There is nothing wrong with skimming a book, reading parts that interest you or that answer certain questions, and then setting that book aside in your reference library for future use.

Don't forget that books are not the only printed material packed with information that could improve your life. We can also benefit from magazines, newspapers, pamphlets, newsletters, signs, backs of packages, and instructions—just to name a few. You would be amazed at how many people never really take the time to read instructions or directions. Yet they often contain some of the most obvious, useful information available. One of the ongoing punch lines in the accounting world is, "When all else fails, read the instructions." For some reason, human beings always seem to ignore the obvious.

Make reading a part of your life. Bask in the power of it all.

What do I read? My reading is divided into two categories—technical and pleasure. I guess you can describe my style as two-fisted reading. One stack of books, newsletters, and miscellaneous printed material contains information that keeps me up-to-date in my business, or in general educates me about the world around me. The other stack makes me *forget* about my business and all that other serious stuff. Murder mysteries and who-done-its. I'm hooked on them. They clear my brain and help me sleep at night so that I don't end up working straight through my dreams.

And, hey, if you really want to get a jump-start on motivation for gaining self-confidence and control of your life, just pick up a biography or two on the lives of women who have "made something of themselves," or who have survived when they were expected not to. Read about their lives, how they succeeded, how they triumphed. I personally love reading about other women. (Did I mention to you that the murder mysteries I read *have* to have a female private investigator in them? An absolute must.) Start thinking about all that *you* can accomplish if you put your mind to it. And then go out and do it.

The Internet

You want information? *Here* you have information. Lots and lots of information. More than you can possibly imagine in one small box—your computer. If you're into computers, the Internet is a great way to acquire all sorts of interesting data, some relevant, tons of it totally irrelevant. If you're not into computers, then the term Internet is probably something you've heard about in the news and have dismissed as too "high-tech" for your lifestyle.

I confess that I personally am not a computer junky, though I use computers extensively to accomplish work in my business. If I had to prepare tax returns by hand, instead of using computer programs, I think I'd close down my office and open up a bookstore. Larry bought me a laptop computer to use while I write this book. It's cute. (He didn't realize at the time that he would end up hauling it to Hawaii and back.) But, ultimately, I do not feel the need to be connected at the hip to my computer or its wondrous possibilities of managing my life. And so, all right, I admit it, I recently bought the book *The Internet For Dummies.* We all have those areas of life in which we're not completely comfortable.

So what exactly is the Internet? According to our ever-so-patient and understanding "Dummies" authors, the Internet is ". . . basically a bunch of computers hooked together somehow . . . all freely exchanging information." Once you learn how to "log on" to the Internet, the information available to you is mind-boggling and, I understand, addictive. So if you are interested in learning how to "surf" the Internet (see, at least I know the language), look around your community for classes. Call the local community college or look in the yellow pages for a local software store. They should have an idea of what classes are currently available.

And don't tell me that you are just too old to learn how to use a computer. My mother, whose first book was published when she was 70 (a book, mind you, that she wrote on an IBM typewriter) and who swore that she had no use for computers, now does all her writing on, you guessed it, a computer. My dad had to finally get his own laptop (I call it his "toy," he claims it's a "tool") because he and my mom were constantly clashing over whose turn it was to use the computer. And I, their CPA daughter, regularly call them for computer advice. "Oh, so *that's* how you put a grid on the page!" Thanks, Dad. So don't tell me you're too old. Get out there and get challenged.

Community College Classes

Speaking of local community colleges, here's a great place to cautiously test the waters of formal education. Community colleges have become much more than mere stepping stones for four-year colleges. They offer a broad spectrum of classes that go far beyond basic general education curriculum. You can find courses on horticulture, investing, golf, computers, finances, watercolor, you name it. And they're cheap. Anyone can attend and you can take as many, or as few, classes as you want. The average age of students in each class varies widely, based upon the subject being taught, but you can now find senior citizens in attendance almost as often as you find the kid right out of high school.

Taking a course at a community college is definitely more of a time commitment than picking up a few books or surfing the Internet, but you get the opportunity to meet other people with similar interests in these classes and you'll enjoy the added benefit of having an instructor available to help put the pieces of the puzzle together. Look into your local college. It could be fun.

Audio Tapes, Video Tapes, and More

There is no denying that we're in a high-tech world. We don't just have record players and hardbound books anymore, much as I love them both. We now buy CDs, play videotapes on our VCRs and listen to books read to us on audio tape. But why fight it? This, too, can be fun if you let it, and can offer you even more options for gathering information.

I recently was wandering through Barnes & Noble and was amazed at the expanse of their audio book section. And while I personally prefer to have a solid book in my hot little hands, apparently a growing number of people enjoy having a book read to them. Maybc it takes them back to their favorite bedtime story that their mom or dad used to read to them at night. My best guess, though, is that people use audio-taped books in their cars, or maybe in their Walkman while exercising, in order to fill in that "down time" while commuting or traveling. Not a bad use of time.

Videotapes are now not just entertaining, they can also be educational. There is a Scottsdale, Arizona-based business called Video Learning Library that offers a wide range of educational videos through their catalog. You can either rent or buy their videos. The range of subjects they carry is vast—finance, health, computers, cooking, travel . . . the list goes on and on.

So don't assume that the road to educating yourself is long and tedious and boring. The types of tools available today are numerous and at times exciting. Ask questions, read, take classes, get on the Internet, watch or listen to tapes. If you don't want to do it alone, ask a friend to join you in your journey. But don't sit back and tell me that you aren't capable of gathering enough information in order to make decisions about your own life. You ARE capable and you can become anybody you want to be.

Where To Find Information

Ask Questions

- Direct your questions to people who are in the position to know the answers.
- Do not apologize when asking a question.
- Listen! (And remember to not be selective in what you hear.)
- Don't forget: THERE IS NO SUCH THING AS A STUPID QUESTION!!!

Read

- Take time to wander through bookstores.
- Build a reference library of books on subjects relevant to your life.
- Remember that you don't have to read the whole book.
- Become familiar with subjects by reading about them *before* you meet with advisors to ask questions.
- Make reading a part of your life. Bask in the power of it all.

The Internet

- Lots and lots of information in one little box—some of it relevant, tons of it totally irrelevant. But it can be fascinating.

Where To Find Information continued . . .

- Don't tell me you're too old to learn how to use a computer. Get out there and get challenged.

Community College Classes

- Broad spectrum of subjects for a minimal price.
- Great place to meet people with similar interests. (And it just could be fun.)
- Instructors can be helpful in answering questions and putting pieces of the puzzle together.

Audio Tapes, Video Tapes, and More

- Don't be afraid to look for new and interesting ways to gather information.
- Fill in the "down time" while you travel, exercise, or just simply relax with audio tapes, video tapes, CDs, or anything else that offers you information on a subject that strikes your fancy.
- Gathering information doesn't have to be "work." Get creative and enjoy the process.

MAKE THAT DECISION!

Tiny, tiny chapter. BIG, BIG IMPACT. So pay attention!

All that information you gather is useless unless you do something with it. And that "something" you need to do is make decisions. Decision making is the key to survival; it is the key to gaining control of your life. You either follow the path that other people place in front of you, or you make your own decisions. And we've already determined that following someone else's idea of what our life should be doesn't work very well.

Decision making should be treated like any other acquired skill. You become good at it by practicing. You learn how by first making little decisions, then working your way up. Think of a small decision, nothing earth-shaking, that you have put off because you simply haven't wanted to deal with it. What kind of information would you need in order to become more comfortable with that subject? Who can you ask questions of? What can you read? Take your time and gather as much information as you need. Don't put pressure on yourself. (And remember to not apologize for asking questions!) Then start to put the pieces together, either in your head, if the subject is simple, or on paper if it has a little more complexity to it. What does this information tell you? In which direction does it lead you? What options does it clearly eliminate?

It is important to remember that except for mechanical, objective decisions such as, "How do I fix the garbage disposal?" or "Which bank will pay me the highest interest rate on my CD?" there is rarely a "right" or "wrong" answer to any question; there is rarely a "right" or "wrong" decision. Life is not that black and white. What you need to determine is which answer, or decision, best suits you and your life. What are you comfortable with? What do you ultimately want? This extremely important personal information is something that only YOU can supply. And it usually is the final piece that makes your puzzle whole. Your wishes, your needs and wants are just as important as any objective piece of information that you find in a book or from an expert. Because it is *your* life you are dealing with.

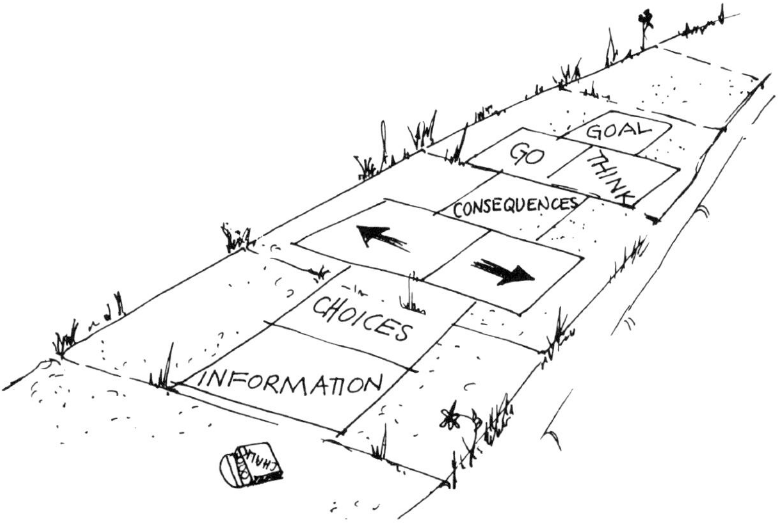

Don't wait for the "perfect" decision to present itself to you. Because it won't. Gather the best information you can, throw in your own personal needs and wishes, and then take the leap. Make a decision. It will feel good. And if you should make what you later consider to be a "less than perfect" decision . . . so what? Learn from it so that the next time you can fine-tune the process. There are very few decisions in life that are life-threatening or irreversible. Remember Rules #8 and #9: *Don't take life too seriously and don't be afraid to try.*

At lunch today, my wonderful friend, client and editor, Barbara McClure, graciously offered herself as an "example" for this chapter, though I initially hadn't planned on using one. I have to admit that our meeting today could not have been more timely. She came to my office to consult with me about a dilemma she was facing: whether or not to incorporate her business. We had talked about this concern on the phone a few times, she had met with her attorney and listened to her input, but she was still unclear as to what to do. The pros and cons were not well enough defined.

She arrived at my office before lunch, purple pad of paper and pen in hand, and started going down a list of questions she had carefully thought about, and written down, before showing up. What were the up-front costs? How did the tax structure work? How would she pull money out of the corporation? On and on, playing with possible numbers, explaining certain tax laws, looking at the most favorable options, until gradually an image started to form for both of us as to the best way to structure her business. Suddenly it made sense; suddenly the best option was clear to her. She had gathered the facts, asked questions, reviewed the consequences of all possible options and then made her decision with confidence. "I'm going to incorporate!!" And so we went out to celebrate.

Facts, decisions, consequences. The basic chain of events that keeps the world in motion. Do not wait for someone else to make decisions for you. You are the only one who has your best interest in mind.

Start with the small stuff and work your way up. Enjoy the sense of accomplishment each time you make a decision. Enjoy the power of being in control.

Make That Decision!

- If you are uncomfortable making a decision, you probably just don't have enough information on that subject.
- Gather relevant information from sources available to you.
  - –Read.
  - –Ask questions.
  - –Review your own personal needs and wishes.
- Which direction does this process take you? What options does it eliminate?
- Now take that leap and make a decision!
- If you make a decision that turns out to be "less than perfect" . . . so what? Learn from it so that next time you can fine-tune the process.
- Remember: There is rarely a "right" or "wrong" answer to any question; there is rarely a "right" or "wrong" decision. What you need to determine is which answer, or decision, best suits you and your life.
- Practice, practice, practice.

THAT TOOL CALLED MONEY

$$$ **Money** $$$ Doesn't that word just jump off the page and grab you? (Okay, so the cute little dollar signs help.) But it's true. Money talks. Money dazzles. Money opens doors and, yes, money makes the world go 'round. And while many of you may not have been fully aware of the significant role that information plays in your life, there is one thing that EVERYONE knows: Money is Power. Yet, what you may not realize is that similar to information, money is best utilized if you think of it simply as a tool. Information is the tool you use to make decisions about your life. Money is the tool used to *implement* many of those decisions.

If your husband traditionally handled the finances in your relationship, you probably haven't had much experience in handling money, so the terms *money* and *finance* may, therefore, be rather intimidating to you. Don't let them be. Let's take the mystery out of money.

Money was created years ago when people got tired of bartering. You know, Mr. Jones needed some grain, but he didn't have any land on which to grow it. What he did have, though, were lots of extra oranges from his trees. So he located Mr. Smith, who had a lot of grain but really wanted some oranges, and they traded. Trading worked, but people eventually got tired of constantly having to locate someone else for an even swap. So money was created. Mr. Jones could now buy grain from Mr. Smith with money and then, in turn, Mr. Smith could take that money and buy a pig, because maybe his wife didn't really care for oranges that much. Money is nothing more than a tool that helps us acquire services and things we need from other people. For that very reason, we also use money as a method of valuing things that we own. These things we own are called *assets.* If we know, for example, that something we own—let's say a painting—is valued at $15,000, what that tells us is that if we sold that painting to someone else, we would then have $15,000 of "buying power" that could be used to acquire other services and items we need or want.

The term *finance* simply means the managing of money. That's it. In other words, it means knowing how to use money as a tool. To improve your life, to act on your decisions, to do whatever you darn well want. Managing your money means deciding how much money to spend and how much money to set aside. It means deciding what investments to put your extra money in: whether to keep it safe, see it grow, or gamble with it. And in order to be able to understand and manage your money, you have to gather information about it. That's right, the general guidelines for understanding and controlling money in your life are the very same guidelines used for any other aspect of your life: You gather information to better understand what you are dealing with, and you use that information to make decisions in order to obtain the desired consequences. You got it. Information, decisions, and consequences within your control. Don't try to make money any more complicated than it is.

Listed below are some fundamental questions about your money that you need to find the answers to so that you can start managing it effectively:

- Where is it?
- How much do you have?
- What type of investments is your money in?
- Are these investments compatible with your lifestyle?
- How much income is your money earning for you?
- What are the tax consequences of the income that it is earning?
- How much do you owe to others?
- How much money do you need in order to live comfortably?

Gathering the above information is called *budgeting and financial planning.* These are things you MUST know in order to maintain control of your life, and in order to make your money work for you. Not knowing what you have, or how to use it, is scary. But . . . gather enough information about your finances and suddenly you've got POWER.

How do you go about getting this information? Back to the basics. Find a good accountant or financial advisor you trust and ask questions. (Don't panic—there are a couple of chapters later in this book that show you how to find and use these people.) Read, take classes, and ask more questions. And remember Rule #5: *You are not a ditz.* You CAN understand what other people are explaining to you. You CAN take control of your finances and subsequently take control of your life. Bookstores are currently inundated with books on finances for women. Take advantage of the surplus, find a few books that work for you, and dig in.

And while the focus of this book is not to dwell on financial strategies, there are two investment guidelines that I am passionate about and want to share with you:

#1: Never invest your money in something you don't understand. Keep it simple. Yes, the world has become a complex, high-tech environment, but that does not mean your finances have to be. Investing does not have to be complicated. If your investment advisor intentionally, or unintentionally, attempts to convince you otherwise, it is probably a good time to look for a new advisor. Do not allow yourself to be talked into an investment you are uncomfortable with. If the rules of the game are too complicated, then it's time to find another game.

#2: If an investment sounds too good to be true, it probably is. Remember our discussion on popular information? Find out about the small print. Don't ever let someone try to convince you that there *is* no small print, no downside to an investment. Because there always is. Look at the negatives as well as the positives of each investment and decision. Don't be blinded by the large, flashy print that only tells you about the good stuff. Honestly look at all sides of an investment BEFORE you put your money into it. Otherwise, you may be in for some economically unpleasant surprises when it is too late to do anything about it.

Don't be afraid of money. Instead, learn how to use it. This is one area where men really have it over most women. They understand the power of their money and they know how to use that power. Now, don't misunderstand me. I'm not saying that men know how to spend money more effectively than women. What I'm saying is that they know how to use the *power* behind their money. Think about it. A man will go into a professional office and say, or imply, "I'm worth 'X' number of dollars, so you'd better treat me right." On the other hand, a woman who hasn't had much experience in the business world or in dealing with money, yet has the same amount of money as the man, will go into the same business and say, "Excuse me, I don't know much about this subject, and I have a few stupid questions. Is there any chance you can find the time to help me?" It doesn't occur to her that she has something those business people would like a part of (her money), and therefore *they* might just have to prove themselves to *her.* Keep in mind, also, that the man, understanding the power behind his money, will more than likely imply that his "X" (we're talking money here) is bigger than it actually is, whereas the woman will understate the value of her "X." Your money can be just as powerful as the next person's money. Look at it as a tool and learn how to use it.

One final note on the subject of money. I am a firm believer that the most important question relating to money is not always "How much is there?" but instead, "Now that I know how much there is, how am I going to use it?" Similar to gathering information, it's a matter of quality versus quantity. As I've stated before, I believe that money should merely be viewed as a means of accomplishing or acquiring a lifestyle of your choosing. Money should not be viewed as an end in itself.

There is a wonderful little book on this subject entitled *Get a Life: You Don't Need a Million to Retire Well* by Ralph Warner. Mr. Warner was one of the founders of NOLO Press, the publishing company that infuriated lawyers back in the '70s by publishing books like *How to Do Your Own Divorce* and *How to Probate an Estate.* These books gave ordinary people enough legal knowledge so that they could do for themselves things that lawyers normally would charge oodles of money to do. (Again: information, money, power.)

The premise of this charming book is simple—you should focus more on how you *fill* your life rather than on how big a retirement nest egg you need. The book offers some great food for thought and it's an easy read. It even contains a few simple chapters on money management. And it really does encourage you to "get a life."

What You Need to Learn About Your Money

- Where is it?
- How much do you have?
- What types of investments is your money in?
- Are these investments compatible with your lifestyle?
- How much income is your money earning for you?
- What are the tax consequences of the income that it is earning?
- How much money do you need in order to live comfortably?
- How much money do you owe to others?

Joan's Investment Philosophy

- Never invest your money in something you don't understand.
- If an investment sounds too good to be true, it probably is.

DIVIDE, SORT, AND CONQUER

Have you ever thought about the fact that it is impossible to solve a problem if you are unable to define what that problem actually is? Or, for that matter, think about how equally difficult it is to make a decision if you are not really sure what you're trying to decide. Yet, unwittingly, it is a consistent habit among women who haven't had much experience in managing their own lives to run all of their unresolved concerns together, and pile up all their problems into one big, muddled, indecipherable mess, making it literally impossible to tell where one problem ends and another one begins.

A perfect example is my client Nancy. The first time I met her, she sat down in my office, opened her mouth, and said something like this: "I just don't know what to do—you've got to help me because the IRS keeps sending me these notices saying I owe them money, but I can't remember if I filed a return for '92 or not because I followed this man to the desert (was that ever a big mistake—I paid for everything) or was it in '91? . . . and now I've lost all my paperwork because I've moved so many times and I just can't believe I'm in this mess and my son, who's an attorney, is living with me now and thinks I should file for bankruptcy, what do you think? . . . but did I tell you how much money I used to make before I met this guy? . . . and I just found out I have to put my mom into a nursing home, but the IRS is sending their notices to an old address because of all my moving, does that help me? . . . and what do you think they'll do if I can't pay it all right now?!"

By the time this woman stopped to take a breath, I was absolutely exhausted! And while I will admit that Nancy is an extreme example, she does demonstrate a very good point: Problems need to be dealt with one at a time. You need to define each one separately, break down the confused pile into individual, smaller concerns and then tackle them, one by one. Joey English, talk show host at KPSI in Palm Springs, told me that her mother worded the same advice quite simply—"How do you eat an elephant? One bite at a time."

Fine, you say, but how do you get started with this big mountain (or should I say elephant) staring you in the face? Believe it or not, it's not that hard. Get a pencil and some paper, find a quiet, comfortable location, and settle in to think for a bit. What seems to be overwhelming in your life? What problems or concerns are just too big to deal with? What areas are just flat-out foreign to you so that you don't even know where to begin? As things come to mind, start writing them down, leaving space between each entry. Take your time. Don't be in a hurry. And keep in mind, this isn't going to be graded; no one else is going to approve or disapprove of your list. So let yourself go and put down anything that comes to mind. There are no right or wrong entries here. Everyone's life situation is different.

You don't know where your money goes each month, and how come you keep getting those late notices when you thought you paid those bills on time? Write it down. The bank says you don't have any money in your account, but you thought you had plenty? Write it down. Your car is making some weird clunking sound but you've never had to take it in to be fixed by yourself before. And you don't want to be taken advantage of, but what if you don't have enough money to pay for a major repair, and how can you tell when it's time to buy a new car? Write it down!

The IRS is sending you notices, you don't know if you filed your tax returns, your son has moved in and thinks you should file for bankruptcy and your mother has to go into a nursing home? For heaven's sake, Nancy, write it down!

Keep in mind that you don't have to accomplish this "unloading" process all in one sitting. When you get tired of the exercise, take a break. Let the list sit there for a while until another entry comes to mind, or until you feel that you have finally touched upon all major, or minor, concerns. And make sure that you're not being selective in what you write down. Don't leave a problem off your list simply because you don't want to deal with it right now. It won't go away and it's time you accept the fact that no one else is going to solve it for you. This is your shining moment to start gaining control of your own life. It is no time to be coy.

Completing your list, or at least consciously going as far as you can with it at this point, will in itself be an accomplishment. You have turned your jumbled thoughts and concerns into something black and white, something tangible. Tangible things can be dealt with. They can be controlled and they can be conquered.

Once all this muck is on paper, we can start playing the break-apart game. Key rule to this game, though, is that you have to pretend that you're looking at someone else's list. Pretend that these are not your concerns, really, they're someone else's. Isn't it amazing how we are able to objectively analyze other people's lives, problems and follies, and see obvious solutions, yet get stuck on our own? It has to do with detachment. With other people's lives, we can stand back and see what is not apparent to them because we are not emotionally involved in the decisions. Emotions have a way of clouding solutions. So look at this list as someone else's list and let's start breaking it apart.

Take each problem on the list and see if it's possible to break it down into smaller, more specific concerns. You'll probably find that this is more difficult than it actually seems at first, simply due to the fact that a lot of these problems and concerns have been lumped together for so long that you may find it hard to differentiate between them; they have all comingled into that muddled, confusing mess we discussed earlier. But most problems really can be broken down into more manageable, less intimidating pieces. It merely takes practice and focus. Let's look at Nancy's overwhelming situation. I would initially break it down as follows:

- Tax returns may not have been filed for one or two years.
- The IRS is sending her notices that have to be responded to.

- Money is owed to the IRS.
- Her mail is not reaching her because she has moved so many times.
- Documents have been misplaced because, again, she has moved so many times.
- Her son is living with her. (Yes, I consider that a problem!)
- She's over her head with expenses and debt.
- Her mother may need to go into a nursing home.

Pretty easy, right? Most of the problems listed above can then be broken down into more specific concerns. For example, I would break down the first three problems, which deal with taxes and the IRS, into the separate years that may be in question.

Once every entry has been broken down as far as you think it can go, it's time to think back to our discussion about information and decision making. Because, you see, problems are really nothing more than situations in which a decision, or a series of decisions, needs to be made in order to make those situations less difficult—or more in tune with how you feel life should be. The next step you need to take is to determine which decisions need to be made, or what action needs to be taken, in order to resolve each concern. At that point you revert back to your basic decision making process we have all come to know and love so well. What information do I need in order to make that decision? Where can I get that information? What does that information tell me? And then, finally, which consequences am I most comfortable with? Step, by step, by step.

So take a look at that list. Take each entry and view it as a mini jigsaw puzzle. What pieces of information (that keep you from making that decision or solving that problem) are missing? Write them down under each entry. Again, don't expect instant revelations on this. Take your time and think, "Okay, if I knew this, this and this, I could figure out that." Then try to fill in the blanks. Once you have determined what information is missing, your next step will be to determine where you can go to find that information. You may be pleasantly surprised to learn that it is simply a matter of asking a few questions of the right people. You may be able to locate some books that give you the necessary input. Or it may be a longer, multi-step process of getting referrals from people you trust, then consulting with professionals who specialize in your area of concern.

But keep in mind that no matter what type of source you end up using for your information, you will be one step closer to making that decision or solving that problem each time you locate a missing piece of the puzzle. I personally find that one of the true joys of making lists on paper is the great sense of accomplishment each time you check an item off. So I encourage you to make a big deal out of it! Go ahead, pat yourself on the back. No matter how small that item is, you're making progress. You've started to gain control.

Write it down, break it apart and check it off. Go slow, take little steps, but stay focused. Solving problems is an acquired skill, just like riding a bike. The more often you do it, the better you get at it. Just remember how to eat an elephant

Divide, Sort, and Conquer

- Problems need to be dealt with one at a time.
- Make yourself a list of your problems and concerns as you see them.
- Break down that list into smaller, more manageable concerns.
- What decisions need to be made in order to solve each concern?
- What information do you need in order to make each of those decisions?
- Where can you get that information?
- One by one, make those decisions. Solve those problems.
- Check them off. Pat yourself on the back. Make a big deal out of it! You're making progress.

(Just remember how to eat an elephant.)

HEY, THEY'RE SUPPOSED TO BE WORKING FOR YOU!

Up to this point, I have primarily discussed what you personally can do, and need to do, in order to gain control of your life. But now I'm going to tell you that nobody can do it alone. We all need a support team, otherwise known as advisors, to back us up in our decision making process, because there is simply too much information out there for any one person to assimilate. So we turn to specialists, people who have dedicated their professional lives to understanding and offering advice in a particular field of information. They can be attorneys, stockbrokers, auto mechanics, CPAs, doctors, gardeners, plumbers, cosmetologists. Anyone you turn to for their knowledge and expertise in areas that affect your life.

Take a look at any number of powerful people, ranging from the president of the United States to, let's say, Jane Fonda. While most of them are well-educated people in their own right, who clearly have their own strong opinions regarding the direction of their lives and the businesses they run, I feel safe in saying that one of the primary traits they share is that they surround themselves with support teams. The teams are usually comprised of people from different areas of business who can offer advice or gather detailed information on problems relating to their particular area of expertise. This allows the "powerful person" to do what he or she does best: steer the boat, run the business, lead the country.

Think of advisors as a kind of human reference library.

My guess is that if you were previously married or, for that matter, still are married, you probably have a support team already set up. You just don't know what to do with them. And if this support team was chosen by your husband and simply passed on to you (as is almost inevitably the case), chances are that it may not necessarily be the team best-suited to your own personal needs.

Selecting advisors is very similar to buying shoes. We all have different shoe sizes, comfort requirements, style preferences and price ranges, and most women don't think anything of taking the time to search for shoes that best fit their needs. Yet, in contrast, a lot of us stick with the same advisors, year after year, even when they are a bad "fit" and even if we are not getting any real benefit from the relationship. Why is this? It has to do with the fact that a lot of us simply don't know how to use advisors; we don't know what to look for. Bottom line, we don't have enough confidence in ourselves to believe that we can be in the "in-control" position when working with an advisor. Yes, you may know that you need an attorney, but you have trouble accepting the fact that an attorney should be meeting your specifications and needs and, ultimately, should be working for you.

One of my clients, Betty, is a well-to-do widow whose husband left her with quite a bit of real estate and a substantial investment portfolio. Betty openly admits that she has always enjoyed being taken care of by the men in her life, and when her husband passed away, she turned most of her assets over to several male advisors, assuming that they would continue on with her best interests in mind. When we met for the first time, several years after her husband's death, she was both discouraged and bitter. She had been having an on-again, off-again affair with her CPA for a couple of years (he was an old friend of her late husband), but the last time he flew out to see her he mentioned that he was planning to marry someone else in a few weeks. In addition to that, she couldn't understand a thing that her attorney explained to her and she didn't know what work he was actually doing for her, yet he kept sending her these exorbitant bills which she went ahead and paid anyway. To top it all off, she hadn't spoken to her financial advisor in years because she simply didn't like him. Yet she continued to pay his firm over $10,000 per year to manage her portfolio.

In my professional opinion, Betty is clearly in a financial position that requires a solid support team of advisors. The problem is, she picked (or kept) the wrong ones for the wrong reasons.

Most professional advisors have, over the years, developed their own particular style and, along with it, a client base that best suits that style. For example, successful businessmen who view themselves with great importance tend to rely on advisors in large, highly visible firms that charge a lot of money for their services and know how to stroke inflated egos. The larger their bill, the more important their clients feel. On the other hand, there are individuals who view themselves as self-sufficient—they just want the work done right for the lowest price, and don't want to pay for a fancy "brand name" of unwanted packaging and advice.

Yet neither of these advisor types are well suited for women who have recently gone out on their own. The needs of these women tend to be totally different from the needs of men who have been making decisions on their own for years.

If you happen to be one of these women, what you need are user-friendly advisors. You need advisors who are there working for you, paying attention to your needs, not the needs of your late husband. If you currently have a list of advisors whom you turn to for guidance, take a look at each one and ask the following questions:

- When you call this person, does he return your calls promptly?
- Do you feel at ease when seeing or speaking to this person?
- Are you comfortable asking him questions?
- Does he seem to welcome and even encourage questions?
- When he answers your questions, do you understand what he's saying?
- Does he really listen to what you have to say?
- Does he take the time to explain the work he is doing for you?
- Does he make it clear that you have options or choices?
- Does he encourage you to make your own decisions?
- And when you finish speaking with this person:
  Do you feel more informed?
  Do you feel better about yourself?
  Do you feel that you are working with someone who is on your side, who enjoys working for you and who has your best interests in mind?

If you can't answer "Yes" to all of the above questions, you should think about looking for another advisor.*

* Footnote: After an initial reading of this chapter, my husband gave me *a terrible* time about using only the pronoun "he," instead of the more politically correct (but cumbersome) "he/she." Personally, I have never been that concerned about "gender-correctness" in what I read or write. I am much more interested in the content. But, please, feel free to substitute "she," "he/she," or, for that matter, "it," if it makes you feel better!

Now let's look at each advisor from a reverse perspective:

- Do you feel intimidated when talking to this person?
- Do you wait and wait and wait for a return phone call?
- Does this person make you feel that you are extremely lucky to have a moment of his valuable time?
- Do you get the feeling that this person is simply trying to sell you something?
- Are your meetings hurried—as if he has something better to do?
- Does he become indignant if you should question his advice?
- Does he say such things as "Trust me, I'll take care of it for you," or "Don't bother your pretty little head over these matters." (Ouch.)
- Does he seem to wish that your husband were still around so that he could be dealing with him instead of you?
- Are you afraid to call this person because he charges you for even the slightest phone call?
- Do you get bills that seem exorbitant or that are for services you didn't request?
- And when you finish speaking with this person, do you feel frustrated and rather stupid instead of more informed and in control?

If you can answer "Yes" to *any* of these questions, then you definitely should look for another advisor!

I can think of many professionals who would be indignant over being put to the above "tests." And for a very good reason. It can take years of education and hard work to become an expert in any field. Once you've put in your time, earned a reputation and title, and people look to you for advice, it's very easy to become filled with self-importance. Unfortunately, that self-importance usually fills the place where empathy and a genuine desire to help others used to be.

Good example: I was recently on a talk show where the other featured guest was a doctor. His first name was Robert. The show's host asked him what he liked to be called: Robert, Bob, Dr. Robert, Dr. So and So. His response was that he would respond to anything but "Mr." He had simply worked too hard earning his title to have it ignored. Talk about an attitude! Heaven forbid that we might meet this man at one of those cocktail parties and not know what he did for a living!

Okay, so let's say that one or more of your advisors flunks the above tests rather miserably, or that you simply do not have an advisor in an area in which you need assistance. How do you go about finding a new one? There are two fairly reliable ways to do this. The first, most obvious way is to contact other women you can relate to and ask them who they use. No different than asking them who does their hair if you like their hairstyle. Then go ahead and ask these same women some of the questions from the first list in terms of how they relate to that advisor. Are you comfortable asking him questions, does he take the time to explain the work he does for you, so on and so on. This will give you good insight into how well this advisor might suit your needs. (It may also give your friend some food for thought about the people she relies on.)

The other reliable way to locate new advisors is to ask professionals, whom you currently rely on in other areas of your life, if they can recommend someone to you. It simply makes sense that if you are already comfortable with one advisor, it is probably because he or she is in tune with what your needs are and would therefore be able to refer a professional in another field whose work style would be compatible with those needs.

Getting referrals from existing advisors also serves another purpose. When one professional refers another professional to an existing client, it is a fair assumption that he respects the other professional and probably shares other clients with him. By having at your disposal a group of advisors who know and respect each other, you, in turn, will get a more well-rounded "team approach" in terms of overall guidance. Very few areas of decision making stand alone; most are interrelated to others. Decisions made about your taxes may rely partly on various legal aspects of your life. Buy and sell decisions relating to a portfolio rely, in part, on your tax situation. Your gynecologist should know what your allergist determined in order to prescribe medication. (You know, your hip bone is connected to your thigh bone . . .) Advisors can serve you best if they are comfortable working with the other advisors in your life.

And while "male-bashing" is by no means the intent of this book, I must honestly interject here that most women who actively go looking for user-friendly advisors usually find that women advisors meet their needs more times than male advisors. The reasons are fairly obvious. Women have been there, women empathize, women are more tolerant. And women clients, in general, are just less intimidated being around other women. I am repeatedly told by new clients how completely frustrated they were with their prior accountants because they either couldn't reach them to ask questions, or were too intimidated to ask questions that they knew would be viewed as "stupid questions." (Which, of course, we all know do not exist.)

Several years ago, one of my clients decided to stop by a SCORE office to get some advice on a product she was starting to manufacture and sell. (SCORE stands for Service Corps of Retired Executives and is a volunteer organization overseen by the Small Business Administration. Retired executives volunteer their time and experience to offer advice to the general community. Good concept.) My client, Susie, raises exotic birds and had started making these amazing toys for parrots out of wood and leather. Not only were they beautiful to look at, but the toys were specifically constructed to meet activity and health needs of these unique birds, and the birds went crazy over them. Susie had started selling the toys at bird "swap meets" (which, I'm told, in the bird community are regular, well-attended events) and was getting a very positive response. So she went to the SCORE office to ask advice about pricing, production and other related matters.

I received a phone call from Susie shortly after her meeting with the SCORE volunteers. She informed me that it had been the most "devastating experience" of her life. The two men she met with made it clear that they thought her business project was frivolous, and her whole approach to it was wrong. They put her down for having actually started selling some of the toys before having done an extensive "break-even cost analysis." They kept pushing her for specific dollar amounts, while she kept informing them that she did not have these figures with her but was just there for some general overview information. When she finally muttered something about needing to talk to her accountant and used a female pronoun, one of the volunteers shot back, "So what's wrong with using a male accountant?" That did it. My clients are *extremely* loyal.

I contacted one of the SBA officials responsible for the SCORE offices, and she admitted that she had heard other stories about problems with some of their volunteers dealing with women looking for advice. She asked if I would send a letter explaining Susie's particular circumstances, which I gladly did. I have not heard of any further situations, so I can only hope and assume that the SBA proceeded with some form of gender training for these older men.

The point I want to make with this story is that most men, at least from the older generations, have taken a well-worn path to business that, until the past few decades, had been unavailable to women. They started in business when they were young, were guided along by the good ol' boy network, and learned how to play the game. In the 1970s and 1980s they started having to deal with younger, well-educated women taking over some of their jobs and breaking into their Rotary Clubs. And now along comes this group of late-blooming women who probably spent the first part of their adult lives raising a family and staying home. They're asking all sorts of basic (stupid?) questions that guys learned the answers to a long time ago, plus they're breaking all of those nice old rules of how and when to do things. Frustrating, very frustrating.

To me, it is an obvious conclusion that late-bloomers are going to break rules or traditions and take paths that are different from the conventional route to business and decision making of any kind. This is simply because our time-frame is different. We started later, we gathered information later, and therefore our jigsaw puzzle is bound to be different. When I went back to school to get my degree and become a CPA, I knew that I couldn't take the traditional path. Most "young things" right out of college headed off to a metropolitan community to gain experience at one of the large national accounting firms. (Back then they were known as the "Big Eight" accounting firms—Price Waterhouse, Arthur Andersen and the likes.) I had two kids, I was established in a community with their school systems, and I just couldn't pack up and move to the Big City. Nor did I want to. So I took the alternate route and went to work for a reputable, large, local firm. While I didn't get to put one of the Big Eight's power names on my resume, I did get the training I needed to become certified and get on with my career and life. To me, that's what it is all about. Different route, same end result.

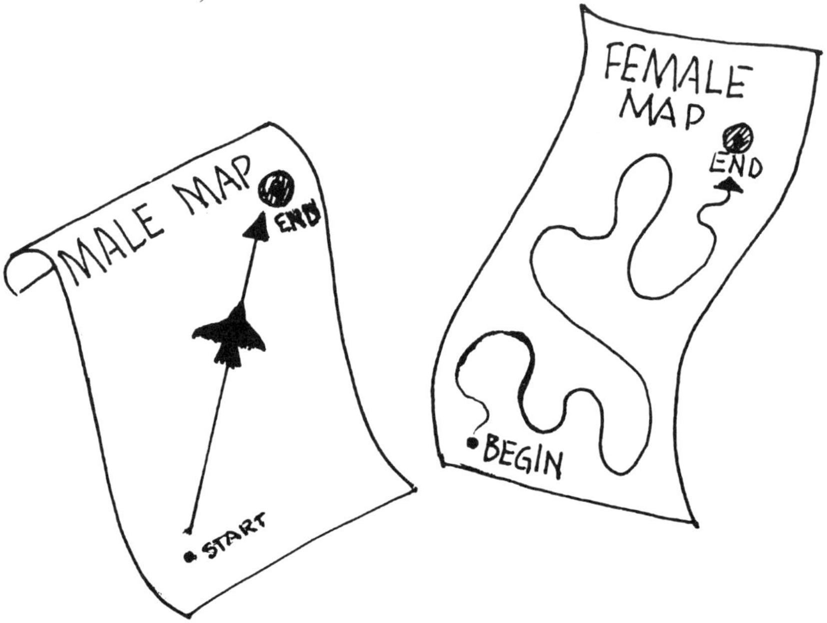

Luckily, there are exceptions to all general rules, and I will openly admit that there are some wonderful male advisors out there who do understand the needs of late-blooming women and who know how to communicate with them. There is a father-son team of financial consultants in my community to whom I refer many of my women clients because I know from experience that they will fill my clients' needs. Conversely, there are many women advisors out there who would sadly flunk the above user-friendly tests.

Now, back to finding one of these user-friendly advisors. Once you've come up with a name or two of recommended advisors, don't merely assume that they will fill your needs simply because they have been referred to you by someone you know. Remember our discussion about information. Everybody's jigsaw puzzle is different. Everybody's needs are just a little different. You should personally meet these advisors to see if they are compatible with your personality and to see if they fit into *your* puzzle.

Don't let yourself be intimidated about contacting these people. Remember that what you are doing is offering them new business, and that is why they are supposed to be there. So simply pick up the phone and let them know you are looking for a new (attorney, accountant, doctor . . .), that So-and-So recommended them to you (very important that you let them know this) and you would like to meet with them to discuss the possibility of doing business together.

This phone call is a good test in itself. If they delay returning your call without a reasonable explanation, are just too busy for the next three weeks, or if they inform you that there will be a consulting fee for this visit, tell them "thank you very much" and cross them off your list. These people are too busy or too full of self-importance and will never give you the attention or service you deserve.

When you finally meet with one or more of these advisors, keep in mind that it is up to them to sell themselves to you, not the other way around. Tell them a little bit about yourself, what your needs are, and then listen to what they have to say. Find out what they charge, what information they require in order to properly assist you, and get a general feel for whether they will pass the two tests above. If you think they will, and you like what they have to say, then you've probably got a winner.

But do not be discouraged if the first one or two professionals you call don't pass these initial tests. There are some very good advisors out there who want your business, who will encourage and support you, and who will assist you in making those necessary decisions in your life. Sometimes you just have to do a little window shopping to find them.

How User-Friendly Are Your Advisors?

Test #1

- When you call this person, does he return your calls promptly?
- Do you feel at ease when seeing or speaking to this person?
- Are you comfortable asking him questions?
- Does he seem to welcome and even encourage questions?
- When he answers your questions, do you understand what he is saying?
- Does he really listen to what you have to say?
- Does he take the time to explain the work he is doing for you?
- Does he make it clear that you have options or choices?
- Does he encourage you to make your own decisions?
- And when you finish speaking with this person:
  Do you feel more informed?
  Do you feel better about yourself?
  Do you feel that you are working with someone who is on your side, who enjoys working with you and who has your best interests in mind?

If you can't answer "Yes" to all of the above questions, you need to think about looking for another advisor.

How User-Friendly Are Your Advisors?

Test #2

- Do you feel intimidated when talking to this person?
- Do you wait and wait and wait for a return phone call?
- Does this person make you feel that you are extremely lucky to have a moment of his valuable time?
- Do you get the feeling that this person is simply trying to sell you something?
- Are your meetings hurried—as if he has something better to do?
- Does he become indignant if you should question his advice?
- Does he say such things as "Trust me, I'll take care of this for you," or "Don't bother your pretty little head over these matters."? (Ouch.)
- Does he seem to wish that your husband was still around so that he could be dealing with him instead of you?
- Are you afraid to call this person because he charges you for even the slightest phone call?
- Do you get bills that seem exorbitant or that are for services you didn't request?
- And when you finish speaking with this person, do you feel frustrated and rather stupid instead of more informed and in control?

If you can answer "Yes" to *any* of these questions, then you *definitely* need to look for another advisor!

WHAT STOCKBROKERS AND AUTO MECHANICS HAVE IN COMMON... AND HOW TO WORK WITH THEM

Ever heard of the White Coat Syndrome? It most commonly refers to a patient's relationship with a doctor. The general concept is that since the doctor is wearing a white coat, he must be right. In other words, it never occurs to most people to question the advice of a doctor because, after all, he IS a doctor! Big mistake.

A doctor, among other things, is also a human being. He makes decisions in exactly the same way that you are learning to make decisions. He gathers information relevant to the situation, reviews it, and then makes a decision or diagnosis as close to the desired outcome as he can. But that doesn't mean he is always right, because very often he's not able to obtain all of the pieces of the jigsaw puzzle. He is, therefore, making the best decision he can make based upon information that is available to him.

The same goes for stockbrokers, auto mechanics, accountants and other advisors in your life. They are not God. They are simply human beings giving you the best advice they can. Period. It is YOUR responsibility to determine if their recommendations are best for you. You are the only person who can ultimately make that decision.

So how do you go about determining if the advice offered to you is the best possible option available for your particular situation? You guessed it. Go back to your basic rules about decision making. You gather more information. You determine if the advice given to you makes sense based upon additional, unrelated but relevant input. As I've mentioned before, you should never rely upon just one source of information for any decision. There are simply too many sources available today to rely on just one. And remember, ultimately it is your responsibility to educate yourself. No one else is going to do it for you.

As a general rule, you should take a "be prepared" approach to all areas of your life in which you are going to be required to make important decisions—areas in which you will more than likely be using advisors. Plan ahead. Locate some user-friendly books on various subjects that affect your life—finance, health, house repairs—books that appear to have chapters on specific topics you may be dealing with. In other words, get yourself that reference library we discussed *before* you get in a panic and don't know where to turn for guidance.

And keep in mind that most advisors charge their clients either by the time spent with them or by the services they perform. Therefore, it makes sense that in order to use the time spent with an advisor most efficiently and cost-effectively, it is important that you go into your meeting armed with a general knowledge of the subjects which are going to be discussed.

As an example, let's take a look at the area of financial investing. As I've stated before, there is an almost overwhelming abundance of easy-to-read books available on investing your money. The first one that comes to mind is *The Wall Street Journal Guide to Understanding Money & Markets.* It is, at most, 1/4 inch thick and has simple little sections such as "What is a Stock?" and "How Mutual Funds Work." Nothing fancy, nothing intimidating. Yet, by thumbing through this type of simple publication, with an easy-to-skim format, you will be providing yourself with a basic foundation on which to develop your discussions with your advisor. If nothing more, skimming through such a book may bring up questions to ask during your meeting. It may also help you understand vocabulary related to the particular topic being discussed. Bottom line, you'll "level the playing field" with your advisors. (That's guy talk for saying that you and your advisors will be having discussions on a more equal level than when they knew all of the information and you knew none.) And that equates to being more in control of the situation and your life.

Now let's bring doctors and auto mechanics into the picture. The key phrase to remember here is "second opinion." Whenever you are given a diagnosis which will ultimately lead to surgery, life-altering procedures or even intense medication, either to your body or to your car, get a second opinion. You take your car in to have the oil changed and they tell you that your alternator needs to be replaced? Get a second opinion. Your doctor tells you it's time to get rid of some little organ that he says your body doesn't really need anyway? Get a second opinion! (And possibly a third.) For that matter, let's go ahead and throw in all forms of "repairmen" into this discussion. Someone wants to do a major repair on the roof of your home? You got it. Get that second opinion.

Whether your back-up information comes in the form of another advisor or printed reference material, you owe it to yourself to gather as much information as possible before accepting advice that will ultimately affect your economic, social or physical well-being. Don't ever be in a hurry to accept or decline the recommendations of the professional you're dealing with. Give yourself enough time to acquire additional facts and data. Once you reach the point where you feel you have gathered a well-rounded range of information, you'll be in a much stronger position to determine if the advice really suits your needs. But keep in mind that if you are still having trouble at this point determining which option is the best for you, it may simply be that right now the best decision is NO decision. Do not allow yourself to be forced into making a decision if you do not feel that the time is right to make one.

On the other hand, if a decision definitely *has* to be made, and you simply can't make up your mind, don't hesitate to turn to someone you personally trust, someone who knows you, to help you make that decision.

It is very important to remember that cold, objective facts are not the only information required when making a decision. As we discussed before, personal facts and personal feelings are also key elements of the decision making process. They are those very tiny pieces of the jigsaw puzzle that pull it all together and make it your own personalized puzzle. You, and those personally close to you, are really the only ones who are fully familiar with these personalized pieces. They were formed by a wide range of experiences which helped to create who you are and document where you've been. You may have had an experience in the past that has had a strong impact on directions that you're clearly not comfortable taking, or your personality may be such that you have a very strong aversion to certain types of risk. (Don't be hard on yourself about this one. Most of us prefer to minimize risk as we get older.) And, whatever you do, do NOT underestimate intuition. While it should not be used in place of facts, don't ignore your own intuition or basic "gut feeling" as a final factor when making a decision. If something just doesn't feel right to you, then don't do it. It's that simple.

So keep in mind that while professionals are an important source of information, their advice should not be taken blindly. You need to educate yourself using other sources of information in order to determine whether their recommendations are right for you and your situation.

Working with an advisor is very different from reading a book, or surfing the Internet. You are dealing with another human being, usually on their terms, within their parameters. You are dealing with personal interaction; you are dealing within a specific time frame. If you do not know how to best utilize this interaction, both your time and money will be poorly spent, and you will end your meeting with no more information than when you entered it. Within this context, I offer you the following guidelines:

- The key word to remember when working with an advisor is BUSINESS. Your advisors are offering you information within the context of *their* business. This is how they earn their living. This is not a social function. You, in turn, though you may not realize it, are also in business. You are in the business of gathering information and services that help you to better direct the course of your life. Do not view your business as frivolous. This is YOUR life. Until you feel a sense of control, there is not one thing more important that you could focus on. Approach your meetings within a business frame of mind.
- Do not tell your advisors your life story. Most of them really do not have the time to hear it, or simply would prefer not to. If there are certain events in your life that directly relate to the subject at hand, then definitely bring them up. But, in general, except possibly at an initial getting-to-know-each-other interview, set aside your personal story, let go of the gory details of your messy divorce, and focus on the business at hand. (Remember Rule #2: *Get on with life.*) Your advisors will respect you for it.
- On the other hand, communicate! Tell them what you want or don't want. Tell them what you expect to gain from your association and what you hope to avoid. They cannot read

your mind. The only way an advisor can meet your needs is if you clearly articulate to him or her what your needs are. So speak your mind.

- Make yourself a list, either mental or on paper, of what it is that you want to accomplish at each meeting or with each phone call. Make sure that each point or concern has been addressed before you end your discussion.
- FOCUS on what your advisor is telling you. If necessary, jot down notes during your discussion to refer to later. Take the time to think about what was said and then, if necessary, ask questions to clarify. You've wasted both your time and his if you leave the meeting without fully comprehending what was addressed.
- I repeat—ask questions! As we have discussed before, these people are there to provide you with information. Take advantage of their knowledge and ask away. Remember, there is NO SUCH THING as a stupid question.
- Do not just blindly accept, or sign, documents prepared for you without reviewing them first with the person who prepared them. Do not just assume that they are correct. Look them over, ask questions, try to get a feel for whether the information in the documents is reasonable and correctly represents what is appropriate to your life and your situation. Yes, documents with legal verbiage can be very, very boring. But they are a necessary evil in the society we live in, and it is YOUR responsibility to yourself to understand what is in them before you "sign on the bottom line."
- When an advisor suggests, or insists upon, providing additional services to you, ask him what the fees will be, and do not just assume that you must accept these services. There are, unfortunately, many, many professionals out there who, without the least bit of guilt, aggressively make work for

themselves. And this habit is not limited to just one type of business. We're talking about doctors, auto mechanics, accountants, lawyers. All professions are guilty of this practice. We have all heard of the doctor who performs just one more hysterectomy so that he can take that European vacation, or the auto mechanic who replaces a perfectly good transmission. Again, it is your responsibility to determine what your needs are. And you do that by gathering additional information, getting second opinions, and accepting responsibility for making your own decisions.

- Finally, do not expect to get something for nothing. Advisors give advice in order to pay their own bills. Repairmen repair things in order to support their own families. It's that basic. Everyone's time and expertise have a value and should be respected. On the other hand, I do not believe in paying for brand name advice or someone's inflated sense of self-importance. And I do not believe in paying for unnecessary or unrequested services. So don't ever be afraid to question an unreasonable bill, but expect to pay fairly for what has been provided to you.

Do not allow life to just happen to you. Do not allow advisors to guide you—all-trusting but unthinking—down the path that they have chosen for you. Decide where you want to go, and use your advisors as an effective source of information that will help get you there.

How To Work With Advisors

- Be prepared before meeting with an advisor. Look through your reference books for a general overview of the subject to be discussed before you get together.
- Approach your meetings within a business frame of mind.
- Do not tell your advisors your life story.
- On the other hand, communicate! They cannot read your mind.
- Make a list, either mental or on paper, of what you want to accomplish before each meeting or conversation.
- FOCUS on what your advisor is telling you. If necessary, ask questions to clarify.
- I repeat, ask questions!
- Do not blindly accept, or sign, documents prepared for you without reviewing them first.
- When an advisor suggests additional services, ask what the fees will be and do not just assume that you must accept these services.
- Do not expect to get something for nothing. On the other hand, do not pay for unnecessary or unrequested services.
- Remember that advisors are not God. They are merely human beings giving you the best information they can.
- It is your responsibility to determine if their recommendations are best for you.

JUST SAY NO

This basic principle is so important that I feel it should have a little chapter all its own. You need to learn to say "No."

Learn to say "No" to your stockbroker. Learn to say "No" to your church, your auto mechanic, your children, your accountant, your doctor, your friends. Learn to say "No" to anyone who is in the position to tell you what to do, influence your decisions, or benefit from those decisions.

I know, I know. This is a tough one. And at first it may sound rather harsh. You want to please those people you care about, and you don't want additional stress or confrontation in your life. But let's take a look at why saying "No" is a necessary element of gaining control.

If you are a person who is uncomfortable with making decisions, your lack of confidence will be openly apparent to those around you. These people, in turn, will more than likely respond to your indecisiveness by either making your decisions for you, or at least encouraging you to move in a particular direction. And as time goes on, a pattern develops: A decision needs to be made, you waver, they make the decision for you. After a while you don't even have to waver; they just go ahead and make the decision without asking for your input.

This protective, take-control behavior of those individuals close to you may, at times, seem comforting and endearing. They care for you, they want to protect you. It feels safe and may take you back emotionally to the comfort zone that your husband or parents created around you. But what do we really have here? A total lack of control of the direction of your own life. And it is important to realize that there may be more than one motive that guides these individuals in their assistance:

#1: Yes, they may genuinely have your best interests in mind.

#2: They may simply be tired of seeing you waver, and just want to get the decision over with.

#3: They may, on the one hand, want to see you make a decision that provides you with the most benefit, but they also may realize that if they head you in one "acceptable" direction, versus another "acceptable" direction, they personally stand to benefit more.

#4: They may simply see you as an easy target that they can manipulate for their own benefit, despite the consequences to you.

The last three motives are probably alternatives that you prefer not to think about. But they exist and are the driving force, either consciously or unconsciously, behind a majority of opinions and advice given to trusting women each day. I have seen this over, and over, and over again.

Take another look at the auto mechanic who replaces a few extra parts that don't really need to be replaced. Think about that stockbroker who sold you those limited partnerships because he got such a HUGE commission on them. (You know, the ones you *still* can't get your money out of.) My personal favorite, of course, is the doctor who told me, at the ripe age of 26, when I knew that I definitely didn't want to have any more children and so had decided to have my tubes tied, that I might as well have a full hysterectomy because I'd end up having everything taken out someday anyway! (I don't mind telling you that twenty years later I am still all in one piece and things are functioning just fine, thank you very much.)

Then there is the church. And your children. They are often key elements in your life that simply cannot be viewed objectively. You are linked to them by complicated relationships in which there is love involved, and often guilt, and spiritual beliefs, and a wanting of acceptance and approval. All these complications and emotions can get in the way of good decision making, especially when there is money involved.

Money has a funny way of affecting people's better judgment. Combine the possibility of financial benefit with some really strong rationalization, and you can end up with some very serious manipulation. The father of one of my clients was a strong Catholic as well as a heavy drinker. His wife passed away a few years before him and he never quite recovered from the loss. (That's right, we must remember that women are not the only ones who suffer from the loss of a spouse.) And while his children did their best to comfort and care for him, he increasingly relied upon visits from the priest of his parish. His children were pleased that their father was receiving this special attention, until he casually mentioned to them one day that the "wonderful" priest had promised him infinite Masses for his deceased wife, and all he had to do was change his will to bequeath the family home to the church. (Keep in mind, so I have been told, that *one* Mass lasts for eternity.) Now, whose best interests did that priest have in mind?

Just the other day, I was driving to a meeting with a new acquaintance who was telling me about his family. His parents had owned a productive farm for several decades when, a few years back, his father was tragically hit by a train and killed instantly. His mother had managed to keep the farm running, but an older brother was now getting involved in the day-to-day management. This man told me how much he and his siblings loved their mother, but they were concerned that someone would take advantage of her. (So far, so good.) Therefore, they were actively trying to convince her that she should never remarry, so that no one could take away her assets. Excuse me? Are we talking about what is best for Mom, or for the "kids"? Are we assuming that Mom is incapable of using good judgment, let alone incapable of learning the legal benefits of wills and trusts? Again, just whose best interests do these "kids" have in mind?

This is not to say that you should never listen to the advice of those close to you. After all, although we discussed in previous chapters that professional advisors are an important source of information when making decisions requiring a degree of expertise, we have also noted that people close to you are often able to give that final bit of personal input to help determine if a course of action really suits your specific needs and lifestyle. But what I am pointing out to you *now* is that you always need to think back to the basic principles behind decision making. YOU are the only one who has your best interests solely in mind. YOU are the only one who understands your exact situation, can put all those pieces of the puzzle together, and can determine if a decision really does feel right . . . or just doesn't feel right.

So, if you have been given advice, or a strong suggestion, on a particular direction to take, if you have gathered additional information from other sources, you've weighed the options, and that direction still just doesn't seem to be right for you, then you need to say "No."

Your stockbroker encourages you to put your money in an investment that, in all honesty, seems to be a little bit too risky for you? Say "No, thank you." You appreciate his input, but you're not comfortable with that investment. Your children want you to move closer to them, but you're not really ready to leave the place you now call home? Say "No, thank you." Tell them you love them, but for now you're more comfortable where you are. Your doctor is encouraging you to take a medication that, according to what you've read, may cause you serious side effects? Just say "No." And ask if he can look for an alternative medication.

Saying "No" will not end your relationship with these people. What it *will* do is make them more aware of the fact that you are in tune with your own needs and well-being. It will let them know that you have the ability to think for yourself, to make decisions for yourself. It will let them know that you are not someone to be manipulated. Ultimately, this new insight into who you really are will allow them to assist you better. And, ultimately, they will respect you more.

Just Say No.

Little word. Big impact.

Learn to say "No."

PUTTING THE PIECES OF THE PUZZLE TOGETHER

It is one thing to realize that you need to make changes in your life. It is quite another thing to actually go ahead and make them. Change can be scary. Success can be scary. We are used to seeing ourselves in a particular role, and it takes courage to change that role. We're used to those knee-jerk reactions we have come to rely on. It's not easy saying, "This is not going to be me anymore."

But the good news is that once you decide to gain control, once you cautiously start making those little decisions on your own, and then those bigger decisions on your own, you are going to feel SO GOOD. The feeling of gaining control of your own life is nothing short of awesome. There is nothing quite like it. It is liberating, it is powerful, it is exhilarating. It opens doors for you that you never thought possible.

I will never forget my own initial awareness of these amazing new feelings. It was when I first went back to school to get my degree. Even though I was married and had two children, I had absolutely no self-confidence. My new classes were at the local junior college about 35 minutes away, and I usually listened to Paul Harvey and the news on my way to school.

One of the first classes I took was Introduction to Business. One day, on the way to class, I was listening to the news, as usual, and the commentator mentioned the change in the country's money supply. The M1 and M2 money supply to be exact. Well, I just about lost control of the car. We had actually discussed the M1 and M2 money supply the day before in my business class and I understood what the commentator was talking about! I was actually learning about things that were relevant to life, to business, and to the economy. I wasn't a dummy, because I understood it!

Now, to be honest, I don't really think that this particular tidbit of information has had any major impact on my life. (And, for that matter, if you asked me the definition of M1 and M2 money supply today, I wouldn't have a clue.) But the point is that the world was opening up to me. I gradually learned all sorts of information that was relevant to my life and my profession, things that other people who were a few steps ahead of me probably took for granted. And I couldn't get enough of it. Suddenly, well, to be honest, gradually, I was able to converse with the guy at the cocktail party. Suddenly, all right, again, gradually, I was able to put the pieces together, and I began to feel more comfortable with making bigger and bigger decisions relating to my own life.

There is also another side effect to gaining control of your life that I should warn you about. You start talking to yourself. Often, quite loudly. You start saying things like "This is SO exciting!" or "Oh my gosh, I understand what he's talking about!" or sometimes just "YES!" But don't be concerned. It feels great. And, oh yeah, you start smiling a lot, too. Sometimes for no apparent reason. Except that maybe the world is starting to look like a better place.

And believe it or not, we have already discussed the steps you need to take in order to get started. That's right. There is nothing magical or complicated about gaining control. There were no mysterious procedures followed by all those women before you. Just a few basic rules and guidelines—to be applied and followed as you learn how to deal with the rest of the world—and you're on your way. The hardest part is simply saying, "I know I can do this." Let's go over what we've talked about:

- Accept the fact that no one else is going to do it for you. You, alone, have the ability to direct the course of your life.
- Concentrate on getting rid of those negative habits that hold you back. Let go of feeling sorry for yourself and don't dwell on the past. Focus positively on all that you can do with the future. Don't put yourself down as being a featherbrain or ditz. You are fully capable of learning what is necessary to gain control of your life. And remember to hold your head up high when dealing with other people. You do not have to apologize for blooming a little bit late. These people are no better or smarter than you. They just got a head start. And, oh yeah, don't forget to dust off your sense of humor, and apply it liberally when needed.
- Start a major campaign to educate yourself. Remember that information is the key to decision making. And making your own decisions is the key to gaining control of your life. Ask questions, read, build up a reference library, take classes. And ask more questions. With confidence.
- Use that information you gather and start making some decisions! Remember, there is rarely a right or wrong decision; it is merely a matter of finding the decision that best suits your needs and wishes. Then practice, practice, prac-

tice. The more decisions you make, the more confident you'll feel about making them.

- Get comfortable with your money. Learn what you have, and what you need, then learn how to use it. How? Ask questions, read books, take some classes. Money is just a tool, so don't let it be more intimidating than it really is. On the other hand, *never* underestimate its power.
- Learn to sort out problems or concerns that you feel are out-of-control or that should be resolved. Don't lump everything together into one overwhelming pile. Break each problem into smaller, more manageable ones. Then determine what decisions have to be made in order to solve these smaller concerns and what information is needed in order to make those decisions. (Yes, always remember how to eat an elephant.)
- Set high standards for all the advisors you work with. Make sure that each one can pass our "user-friendly" tests. If they can't, keep looking until you find advisors who *are* compat-

ible with your needs, then take advantage of their expertise and support. But keep in mind that they are not God. You, ultimately, must take responsibility for each decision made relating to your life.

- View managing your life as a business, and respect the fact that your advisors are working with you in the context of their own business. Approach them with specific questions in mind, and focus on what they have to tell you. Do not be afraid to ask them to reword their answers if necessary. Combine their advice with other sources of information to determine what decisions and course of action are best suited to your life.
- Do not be afraid to say "No."

Life is one enormous jigsaw puzzle, and we never know what pieces are going to be handed to us. But with the tools provided to you in this book, and the determination that you are now ready to take charge, you will be able to handle whatever passes your way. Come join the sorority of other women who have been there, and start *thriving* beyond Happily Ever After.

SO WHAT ARE YOU GOING TO DO WITH THE REST OF YOUR LIFE?

Here we are, you and I, at the end of this little journey together. I have given you my all. I have shared with you my own experiences and growing pains, and the experiences of other women just like us. I have laid out before you, as clearly as I could, the basic guidelines and framework for surviving and thriving beyond Happily Ever After. I have shown you that you are not alone, that millions of other women before you have taken this same path towards a more confident, in-control life. The rest is up to you.

Have I been able to reach you? Have you begun to realize that there is a different way to approach life, a way that allows you to choose the direction you want to go, a way that opens up all sorts of new possibilities that you didn't really believe existed? I genuinely hope so. Because now it is your turn.

It is your turn to look within yourself and decide who you want to be. It is your turn to find the strength to take those first steps that will change, forever, your relationship with the rest of the world. And it is your turn to realize that no one else is going to do it for you.

Think back with me, one last time, to when you were young and life was so very simple. Remember dreaming about who you wanted to be? Remember envisioning that "grown-up you" relating to the world outside? Remember those feelings of hope and anticipation? You can get those feelings back again—today. Because now it is time to set aside the past and think ahead to the future. Just what *do* you want to do with the rest of your life?

Reach within and acknowledge what makes you happy. Locate within what makes you feel fulfilled. What unfulfilled accomplishments would make you feel content in the knowledge that you have lived life? Now . . . go ahead and make these hopes and dreams your new goals.

Goals are a universal, yet intimate, part of each of our lives. Goals are what keep us moving forward. They are what keep us looking towards tomorrow instead of focusing on the past. A goal may be as simple as spending more time with your grandchildren or buying a new car. It may be as ambitious as getting a college degree, writing a book, or moving to a place you've always wanted to live. You should have short term goals and long term goals. Short term goals are those instant gratification things that reinforce in us our ability to complete something. Long term goals are the things that make us feel that we are making something of ourselves, that we have lived. Make a list of your goals and keep it close by. Check off goals you accomplish, and enter new goals as they come to mind. Have some fun with your list, and remember not to take life too seriously. Allow your goals to guide you towards better control and fulfillment of your own life.

One final comment. Do not expect the insights in this book to turn you into a completely new person. It won't happen. We are all, instead, comprised of a series of layers. Life's experiences are what have created these layers. And what you are doing now is simply adding additional experiences onto who you already are. The bottom layers never really go away, even though they may be securely covered over by your new experiences, renewed confidence, and knowledge. Your initial insecurities, reactions, and self-doubt will inevitably resurface from time to time. But instead of letting them get you down, embrace them as reminders of how far you have come. Use them as a catalyst to reach out to other women and say, "Come join us."

So, my friend, with these thoughts in mind, just what *are* you going to do with the rest of your life?

ABOUT THE AUTHOR

Joan Busick is a certified public accountant in Palm Desert, California. She has earned a solid reputation as an "accountant for women" through her years of experience working with, and giving seminars to, women in all phases of life. She writes an ongoing column for the monthly publication *The Desert Woman,* and is a regular guest on local radio talk shows. Joan resides in the desert with her husband Larry Goodwin, and their cat, Bonkers. She may be contacted at: P.O. Box 12933, Palm Desert, CA 92255.